The Secret of the Lord

"*The Secret of the Lord* is for women who want to dig deeper and reach higher. It is for women who want their souls stirred and their spirits ignited. It is for women who want to be called to something greater than the ordinary. *The Secret of the Lord* is for me . . . and you."

—DONNA VANLIERE,
New York Times Best-Selling Author, *The Christmas Blessing*

"God wants us to be free of the masks of pretense. We reveal His glory with unveiled faces. When I decided, with fear and trembling, to take down my mask of pretending that I had it all together, I found a trusted friend, and we became partners in the process. We didn't really know what we were doing only that God was leading us. I wish I had had a copy of Dannah Gresh's *The Secret of the Lord*. Dannah has written a biblically sound guidebook that gently leads us through the process that brings true freedom and healing. I recommend it to you."

—RUTH B. GRAHAM,
Author of *In Every Pew Sits a Broken Heart*

"All of us can relate to the issue of wearing a mask that doesn't match the heart. Dannah is compassionate in her writing and encouraging to those that find it nearly impossible to confess the sins that cause us shame and guilt."

—ANNE BEILER,
Founder of Auntie Anne's Pretzels

"God taught me so much through reading *The Secret of the Lord*. I learned through the process of dying to self and relinquishing the intense control I struggle to hold on to, the masks I longed to protect and guard . . . came down one by one—perhaps the greatest being the lie that my sin somehow is greater than God's mercy and forgiveness.

The Lord is patiently teaching me how much he adores me . . . longs for me . . . pursues me . . . in the midst of my most sinful, weak, and broken places. His voice tenderly whispers, "I have only outrageous love for you," when I fall flat on my face . . . my pride . . . my fears. Perhaps the most extraordinary discovery of all is that I am simply a broken woman . . . needing to forgive myself as much as my neighbor. I am discovering that the least of the brethren of Jesus—the one I can help the most by forgiving, the one who needs my love and compassion the most—is perhaps me.

Yes, God continues to write each of our stories. They are tales of unfaithful, broken women rescued and loved by a very faithful and passionate God."

—TAMMY MALTBY,
Cohost of Emmy Nominated *Aspiring Women* and Author of
Lifegiving: Discovering the Secrets to a Beautiful Life

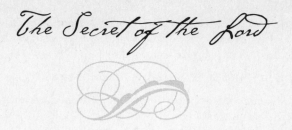

The Secret of the Lord

*The Simple Key That Will
Revive Your Spiritual Power*

BY DANNAH GRESH

NELSON BOOKS
A Division of Thomas Nelson Publishers
Since 1798

www.thomasnelson.com

Published in Nashville, Tennessee, by Thomas Nelson, Inc.

Nelson Books titles may be purchased in bulk for educational, busi-ness, fund-raising, or sales promotional use. For information, please e-mail SpecialMarkets@ThomasNelson.com.

Library of Congress Cataloging-in-Publication Data

Gresh, Dannah.
   The secret of the Lord : the simple key that will revive your spiritual power / by Dannah Gresh.
   p.   cm.
Includes bibliographical references.

ISBN 0-7852-1235-3 (pbk.)

1. Gresh, Dannah.   2. Christian women—Religious life.   3. Bible. O.T.   Psalms XXV, 14—Criticism, interpretation, etc.   I. Title.

BV4527.G75   2005
248.8'43–dc22   2005017668

Printed in the United States of America
06 07 08 09 RRD 5 4 3

To Wisdom, my brave Zambian brother in Christ
who is the secret of the Lord

Contents

Acknowledgments   xi

An Invitation to Revival   xiii

PART ONE: PREPARING FOR THE SECRET

Chapter 1   Prepare to Re-Dream   3

Chapter 2   Prepare to Awaken the Enemy   17

PART TWO: THE SECRET OF THE LORD

Chapter 3   A Prescription for Loneliness   29

Chapter 4   Lie #1: "I'm All Alone Here!"   41

Chapter 5   Lie #2: "There's No One I Can Talk To"   53

Chapter 6   Lie #3: "God Has No Use for Me Now"   67

PART THREE: THE FEAR OF GOD

Chapter 7   The Fear of Man   81

Chapter 8   The Fear of God   93

Chapter 9   The Reward of Fearing God   105

PART FOUR: THE COVENANT

Chapter 10   Yada! Yada! Yada!   119

Chapter 11   Covenant Power   133

PART FIVE: SHARING THE SECRET

Chapter 12   The Hem of His Garment   149

Chapter 13   Walking with the Maskless   159

Chapter 14   Revival   169

Endnotes   177

Acknowledgments

I didn't set out to write this book, but I'm so excited that this is where it ended up. The plans I had for one were quite different. I have a lot of people to thank for helping me find this end result.

First, and always, thank you to my precious God. I was driving down the road one day, pondering a title for my book proposal, when the Holy Spirit brought Psalm 25:14 to mind. "The Secret of the Lord," I said . . . and then I wept. This verse has been so powerful in my life these past three years, and embracing the beauty of it excited my heart. The direction toward this title was overwhelming, and it was the first redirection toward focusing entirely on this verse. And it is no small miracle when the title an author gives to the work still stands after all the other experts have had their say!

Second, thank you to Brian Hampton, my editor at Thomas Nelson. He saw the form of this book in the glob of wet clay that I first sent to him months ago. He gently and patiently invited me to keep molding. I'm so glad I did. His kind direction was a powerful tool in my life. Thanks also to Jonathan Merkh, my publisher, and the rest of the team at Thomas Nelson, including Paula Major, Belinda Bass, Brandi Lewis, and Jana Burson.

Thanks to Wes Yoder, my agent from Ambassador Speakers Bureau and Literary Agency, and Cheryl Dunlop, whose copyediting has forged a sweet friendship.

On the home front, this year I desperately leaned on the support of Nadia Kolosev and Lindsay Williamson. Without their love and support, I could not have managed my home and had the privilege of writing this book.

Just in case you're getting bored with this page, here's a tip. Get one of singer and songwriter Sara Grove's CDs. Sara has never met me but has been the secret of the Lord to me countless times as my heart was soothed by the powerful and transparent words in her songs. Thank you, Sara. I don't know how I could have endured the most painful year of my adult life without your voice mingling with mine as it mixed with tears of hope and courage in my car.

Finally, thank you to my fantastic husband who believed in this book, sought out Wes, and helped me step out into new territory. But most of all, Bob, you've been my own private reservoir of the secret of the Lord.

The secret of the LORD is with them that fear him;
and he will shew them his covenant.

—PSALM 25:14 KJV*

t was the sweetest kiss I'd ever witnessed.

Later, I stood in the receiving line, wanting to completely absorb the moment. The romance. The joy. The anticipation.

I approached the groom, a stranger, with stories of the bride running through my head. Let's see, Lauren was fifteen when I met her at a slumber-party-style retreat. She'd known the Lord Jesus personally for only three months. Her newfound desire for God was a fiery pas-

---

* I don't normally work from the King James Version. Psalm 25:14 is so richly worded in the original Hebrew that it was difficult to translate. As a result, you can place multiple versions of the Bible side by side and find that this verse sounds drastically different. As I searched for the best version of Psalm 25:14, this became my favorite simply because it is so beautiful.

sion. Sometimes it burns to touch such heat. And burn it did. Lauren found that to touch it, she had to walk away from a high school sweetheart—one who desired to rob her of God's precious gift of virginity. We cried together . . . a lot. But together we pressed forward into the promise that God's best for her was yet to come and when it did there would be no pressure to mar the great gift of sexual passion.

She met Kevin in college. They were "just friends." He soon shared with her the dream to kiss his wife for the first time at the wedding altar . . . a sacrifice of holiness to God. Lauren laughed and wished him luck in finding that girl!

I don't have to imagine that their first kiss was sweet and sensual all at once. I was in the audience, wringing out my tissue. And most mystifying to many who miss this chance, the sweet and sensual combined into holiness.

Moving forward in the reception line, I approached Kevin. We grasped each other's hands and looked into each other's eyes for the first time. I felt I was with a close friend.

"You must be Dannah," he said.

"I am," I replied.

"I just want to thank you," he said.

No other words needed to be spoken. I began to cry great tears of celebration. Moving to the side, I stood vainly attempting to compose myself. But composure, after all, can be pride, and I had none at this moment. For in my mind was another fifteen-year-old girl. A girl who didn't walk away from the lustful passion of her high school romance. A girl who knew not the lively burn of following God, but regretted the emptiness of her life without it.

A girl named Dannah.

The return to a full life was long. Filled with fear. Saturated in shame. Until the shame gave way to confession. The confession to healing. The healing to comfort. And what can one do with such comfort but share it? It is too much to keep.

God soon directed me to take off the garb of the professional world and hang out at high school girls' slumber parties. He invited me to rip off my mask of perfection and share the ugliest sin of my life. I found a rich and vibrant new faith in my God. At no moment was that truth more profound than at this one as I stood near this beloved bride and her new groom. It was too overwhelming. There was nothing in me to compose.

When the glory of God touches the ugliest part of your life and uses it, there is no pride.

Only awe.

As a child, I feasted on the stories of Christian missionaries. I eagerly anticipated my congregation's annual missions conference where I'd meet these men and women who were like heroes to me. I had an immediate and intimate connection with each one. I wondered if they knew this kind of friendship everywhere. I could sit for hours, mesmerized by their great adventures. Theirs were stories of the miracles of God. I loved their faith.

I wanted a faith like that. I wanted a deep love for other believers that caused me to connect with them no matter where life's road took me. I wanted stories that made others hunger for Jesus to fall from my lips.

With enthusiastic optimism at the tender age of eight, I committed my life to follow in the footsteps of these men and women of faith. I didn't waste one day pursuing the adventure. By the time I was fifteen, I was a summer missionary and so crazy in love with Jesus that I felt butterflies in my stomach when I prayed.

Every Wednesday, I had to call another summer missionary from our spring training team. It was required that we pray together, by phone, for an hour. We *really* prayed for each other. We talked about struggles in our homes, temptations we were facing, and even horrible sin we had known and needed healing from. We laid it all out. Of course, we also shared wonderful stories about the little children in underprivileged neighborhoods with whom we'd prayed to begin a real and intimate relationship with Jesus Christ that week. That's when I really got butterflies! Though separated by miles, we intimately knew each other. I was finding that amazing bond that I had when I was in the presence of those missionaries. I was on my way to being what I'd dreamed of. I was sure of it.

Then, I got lost.

It happened on a wooded path. It was the autumn that followed my first summer as a missionary. A moment of lust and passion that I thought myself incapable of overtook me. It seared my heart with regret and shame.

I eventually got out of that relationship, but I wasn't the same.

I withdrew from my youth group. I hid from my precious Jesus. I looked around me every Sunday. *Should* I tell someone? *Who* could I tell? I looked from face to face to face and realized that I wasn't as pure or as righteous as any of these. I soon made my choice. No one would know. I slapped on a mask of happy perfection to match the other smiles I saw in my little congregation.

Masks of Perfection

Little did I know that many of those smiles were merely masks of perfection too.

These masks are nothing new. C. S. Lewis wrote about them in 1933 when he penned *Pilgrim's Regress*, an allegory about a boy named John. At the beginning of the story, a masked advisor, supposedly the wisest concerning spiritual matters, lists all the rules John must live by and asks if he has broken any. For a brief moment he removes the mask and encourages John that, rather than confess, he had "better tell a lie, old chap, better tell a lie. Easiest for all concerned." Then, he pops the mask back onto his face and goes ranting on once again about the rules.[1]

> *"Unless we sense that we belong to each other with masks off, the vibrant church of today will become the powerless church of tomorrow."*[2]
> —LARRY CRABB

Lewis could have been writing about my life. I was convinced my mask made me look as good and as happy as everyone else. That's what the enemy led me to believe. In reality, it just weighed me down and acted as a barrier to intimacy.

It isolated me.

That isolation resulted in a lack of spiritual power in my life. By the time I was twenty-five, the pain of my sin was something I still pondered nearly every day though it had happened years before.

My new marriage caused a familiar question to rise up in a new way. "*Should* I tell him?" My faith had settled into a routine and steady observance. I submitted to spending Sunday mornings as a spectator. My husband and I joined a small group where the most intimate request we prayed for was the Smiths' "need" for a new car.

Oh, I "served" God, signing up to do this or that, being careful in all my busyness to keep my mask of perfection properly in place. I was one of the "names" at church. I was there every Sunday and many evenings. In between my acts of service, I vacillated between mild discouragement and deep depression. I was nearly always exhausted.

In the reality of this routine faith, I *still* wanted to be like those missionaries. I craved real, intimate friendships and stories of fantastic faith. I wanted others to hunger for God when they saw Him in my life. I often asked God to use me in the lives of women. He didn't. I now know why. How could I help others be transformed if I didn't feel the transforming power of God myself?

The problem's source was somewhat vague to me. Yet, I knew what imprisoned me from experiencing intimate friendships and stories of faith—my shame. I pleaded with God for freedom.

Then, one day God began to answer my pleas, but not quite as I'd imagined. I was driving down the highway with my brand-new baby girl, Lexi, listening to a radio program about teen sexuality. How often I'd prayed for her not to know this same pain I carried. My ears were in tune.

"What's the number one thing on a teen girl's mind when she's talking to her mom about sex?" asked the interviewer.

"Mom, did you wait?" came the answer without hesitation. I

pulled to the side of the road and collapsed. I felt the pain in full measure for the first time. How would I ever answer that question with this mask of perfection stuck on my face?

I didn't even think about it. I knew that my husband was the first one I had to tell and that it had to happen right away, before I slipped back into my closet of fear. I remember it as the most terrifying and emotionally wrenching three hours of my life. Him waiting. Me crying. Him looking fearful. Me certain he'd withdraw and be hurt and angry. Him holding me. Me pulling away. I will never forget the feeling of those words of confession coming out for the first time. I'd lived so long with the burden of isolation that the only thing left was for me to dare to believe that God's forgiveness was as big as He said it was.

And it was.

In my husband's arms, I felt it.

It was like a cleansing—a spiritual rebirth. The mask had been torn. I didn't realize it then, but it was the beginning of my personal revival.

Spiritual Comas

John 10:10 says that Jesus came that we may "have life, and have it to the full." Many believers do not know such abundant life. Rather, as I once did, they know life from a depressed or an inactive spiritual point of view. They're spiritually alive, but barely. It's like being in a spiritual coma. They go through the motions of Christianity, but they find themselves wondering why they're as depressed and discouraged and exhausted as their non-

Christian peers. Do you know what I'm talking about? Do you need to be revived from your spiritual coma?

Merriam-Webster's Eleventh Edition defines *revive* as "to live again," "to return to consciousness or life" or "to restore from a depressed, inactive, or unused state." For nearly ten years, I existed in that place. It was one of such heaviness. Each day, I was filled with an ache so deeply embedded in my being that I preferred sleeping to being awake. And when I was awake, I felt as if I were covered in a cloud that created a mental state of existence somewhere between confusion and numbness. I was so held back by my shame that it was as though I were spiritually unconscious. My spiritual pulse was quite weak.

What's your spiritual pulse like? Are you living in the great adventure and miracles of God? Or are you closer to living in a spiritual coma? Do you long for something more . . . something deeper?

If you're longing for something more, you're far from alone. Since 1991, the percentage of unchurched women has risen from 18 to 30 percent.[3] Today's overextended woman has no patience for a powerless, impersonal church experience.

Among those who are sticking it out, half are still desperately trying to find a few close friends.[4] Twenty-five percent of those say they feel discouraged and depressed.[5] They're stuck behind masks of perfection. Are you one of these women? Has your faith settled into a routine and steady observance? Is there a mask of perfection plastered to your face? Do you wonder how you'll ever transform the lives around you when you cannot even feel the transforming power of God for your own life?

It doesn't have to be this way.

Do you dare to believe there is something more?

FROM POWERLESS TO VIBRANT

These pages are the best and worst of my life. I should probably tell you that most of my days are lived just in the middle—they're not great or bad, just average. My husband, Bob, and I have been married for sixteen years and seem to be settling much too quickly into older bodies. (Where on earth does this cellulite come from?) We have two fabulous kids—Robby, who's fifteen, and Lexi, who's twelve—whom I help with homework and drive all over town. And we just added Stormie the Labradoodle to our family.

Right here—in the middle—I'm living a vibrant, far-from-average adventure of a life. Just a few years ago I had a husband, two kids, and a cocker spaniel. Funny, my life then was so different. I was powerless. The difference—not found in the basics, in the circumstances—is in my living a mask-free life, and it is tremendous. Let me show you how *your* life can become vibrant, too!

REVIVING YOUR SPIRIT

The psalmist King David wrote a powerful prescription for the masked perfection and powerlessness believers are experiencing today. Psalm 25:14 KJV reads, "The secret of the LORD is with them that fear him; and he will shew them his covenant." One glance at that verse doesn't suffice. You have to look deeply into the Hebrew language to find its carefully veiled power for your life. To truly uncover its power will take some time. We're going to look at it phrase by phrase and word by word. It's *that* packed with power. Once you get this verse into your life, you'll find the faith and friendship you've been searching for.

What is the secret of the Lord? This isn't a secret as you or I would know a secret. It's a rich Hebrew phrase that is difficult to translate into our language. Its most literal translation would be "the people of God who are friends." It's us. But we can't stop there, because the Hebrew language describes these people. They are a tight-knit group of intimate friends with unconditional trust; a circle of friends among whom weaknesses, strengths, successes, and failures are shared. Within this circle, our sins are confessed and forgiven. Our masks of perfection are removed. We aren't afraid to tell our stories, and we are truly known. The secret of the Lord is the intimate friendship that exists between believers. I can't wait to have the power of the secret of the Lord unleashed in your life!

It's real.

It's life-changing.

It's reviving, and it's the door to spiritual power.

I've found it. Do you want that too? Come. Discover the secret of the Lord.

❧— IT'S YOUR TURN —❧

If you really want to work the truth of this book into your life, you'll need a journal. Journaling is one of the most powerful spiritual disciplines that you can master. I've practiced journaling for so long that I have stacks of handwritten books about my life in our attic. I cannot tell you how many times those books have been lifelines. Just when I think I'm not progressing on an issue or not sensing God's presence, I look back through recent pages, and I can see God's hand in my life! I see answered prayers, loud words of wisdom from the Bible that seem to be carved out just for me, and hallmarks of progress. You'll find the same thing if you simply write down your thoughts, feelings, and fears.

Besides, who do you think is keeping you isolated, lonely, and discouraged? John 10:10, the verse where we find the promise of full and abundant life, begins, "The thief comes only to steal and kill and destroy." Satan does not want this for you. It'll be what *you* write in the days to come that knocks him between the eyes. As you process God's truth and savor favorite verses we study, you'll be able to see life transformation taking place in your own precious words.

For your assignment today, I just want you to write a flow-of-consciousness entry on this question: Are you wearing a mask? Look deeply into your heart. Is there someone who knows your deepest fears, failures, and sins? In your journal today, talk to God frankly about it and begin to ask Him what to do with it. Then, stop right there.

My honest advice is that I wouldn't take the mask off *just yet*. I've seen some people crash and burn in the process of stepping into the secret of the Lord. I'm convinced there's some wisdom to be applied in the process.

We need to begin with some foundational expectations. I hesitate to call them warnings, so let's call them promises. There are two things I can promise will happen as you become aware of the secret of the Lord. So before we dive in together, let's look at what you can expect along the way. In the next two chapters, we'll examine my two promises and get you prepared to encounter them.

PART ONE

Preparing for the Secret

CHAPTER ONE

Prepare to Re-Dream

Good and upright is the LORD;
therefore he instructs sinners in his ways.
He guides the humble in what is right
and teaches them his way.

—PSALM 25:8–9

It had been only weeks since I'd allowed my husband to see me. To really see me. All of my hurt and shame were now on the table to love or reject along with my strengths and gifts.

And he loved me still.

It was freeing like nothing I've ever known. The fear was gone. Until . . .

"Dannah, we have a problem, and we've prayed about it," said one of my church's deaconesses. "We think you might be the solution."

She had my ear. I leaned in to listen.

"There is a teenager that wants to attend the women's retreat this year, and we're not comfortable with that," she explained. "We'd like to offer the teen girls a retreat just for them. That's where you come in. Since we've heard such good things about your corporate training and *you're young enough to be 'cool' to them, we'd like you to consider being the facilitator."*

I resisted it, but that uncontrollable smile of pride began to turn up the corners of my mouth.

"We feel really strongly about the subject," the woman continued.

"What subject?" I asked.

"Sexual purity," she said matter-of-factly. She had no idea she'd just stabbed a stake into my heart.

It would be nearly a month before I finally agreed to do it, and that was only so I would not have to tell them why I felt so unqualified.

It seemed that the mask had only been torn and not actually removed. I patched it up a bit and determined that no one but my husband would ever know my sin.

I'm not the only woman to have the mask of picture-perfect Christianity cloud my view. It seems that the pattern of women is to withdraw into our own silent worlds of pain rather than let our sin or pain be seen by others. World-renowned Bible teacher Beth Moore confesses,

My heart used to resemble a condemned property. Oh, I kept a fresh coat of paint over it so that no one would know, but I knew it was a wreck on the inside. I even turned the sign over on the other side and wrote: Fun Person Who Has It All Together . . . As Long As You Keep Your Distance and Don't Look Closely.[1]

After years of hiding intense pain caused by the sin of others against her and her own sin, Beth took off her mask. She soon wrote a Bible study called *Breaking Free,* which she touts as her testimony of overcoming the bondage of the enemy. In that place of bondage she knew loneliness and depression to the point of needing to completely transform her mind. *Breaking Free* shares the powerful process she went through to rise from the massive heap of isolation in the church to become one of the most respected Bible teachers of our day. She's selling millions of books and Bible studies and speaking to stadiums full of women. Her life changed drastically when she took off that mask.

For me, moving from a place of broken isolation to exciting usefulness began with that simple confession to my husband and continued with God-appointed moments of healing and restoration. I now have stories of great adventure and miracles of God. Now, teenage girls watch my faith like I watched as a child the faith of those precious missionaries. Hundreds of thousands of teen girls have read one of my books. Many more have been to one of my events to learn how to live lives of purity. Please understand that I don't say this to brag. I'm just so in awe of what God has been able to do with this once pathetic, isolated sinner that I can't help but share it.

The first thing you can expect, if you choose to apply the principles of this book, is that God will redirect your life. This redirection may be a gentle adjustment of where you're already headed, but more likely you've picked up this book because you desperately desire change. The change God calls for may be drastic. You may have to reluctantly release old dreams to embrace something far better.

You might face a crisis of belief—a crisis not unlike that of the followers of a carpenter with the precious name of Jesus. A carpenter that these followers had dreamed would change the meaninglessness of their lives. A carpenter they thought would overthrow the evil governing them. But there they stood . . . watching Him die. Go with me to that day. I think there's something there for us as we face our own quest to find God's reviving power for our lives.

The Disciples Stood at a Distance

The empty eyes of Roman soldiers gaze upward. Their callous hearts are so hardened by the hideous, torturous death that they engage in a game. There at the base of the wooden cross, in their great glistening helmets, they cast lots for the clothes of the dying. They seek tokens of His horrific death.

Imagine picking up the paper today to read that last night a terrible murder was committed by a local gang. At the site of the murder, a few of the gang members played cards to see who would get to take the victim's watch home. Such was the character of those whose hands did the work of Christ's crucifixion.

The soldiers aren't the only ones watching Christ's torment. There's a large gathering of critics who've come to leer and jeer. They've come for the sport of it, engulfed in morbid fascination.

Seems odd in our intellectual, modern Western culture that some would come out of morbid curiosity. And yet, it happens here. "If it bleeds, it leads" is a timeworn TV newsroom cliché.

6

One suicide bombing image complete with bloodstained and torn bodies is far more likely to hit the front pages than hundreds of pieces of good news from the day. We're engulfed by morbid fascination, explaining why extremely violent movies such as 1960's *Psycho* or 1994's *Pulp Fiction* earn the distinction of being on the top 100 movies of all time. Many of us simply can't resist seeing with our own eyes what all the gruesome buzz is about. Such was the crowd that watched Christ's crucifixion. Curious, mindless by-standers.

And, oh yes, there was one more group of people there that day. The followers of Christ. Wait. Just where are they? Oh, there they are standing "at a distance," according to Luke 23:49. The crowd is pressing in on all sides of them. In their defense, they were physically and emotionally depleted, confused, and utterly disappointed. I can just imagine the thoughts whirling through their minds as they stood in the midst of the crowd.

How can this be the plan, God?

How can such evil triumph if He is really who He says He is?

What on earth have I gotten myself into?

And so, there they stood, blending in with the curious crowd.

Jesus gazes down in love. "Father, forgive them," He says, "for they do not know what they are doing" (Luke 23:34).

It's so easy to read those words and direct them only at the soldiers. We might even direct them at the crowd. I think that would be a mistake.

My friend, I think they were for the soldiers, I think they were for the crowd, but I also think they were for His followers.

I think they were for me.

I think they were for you.

"Father, forgive her. She doesn't know what she's doing."

Are We Standing at a Distance?

Truly we live in an age of evil. Truly we live in an era of curiosity. And truly we, His followers, are physically and emotionally depleted. And many of us are confused and utterly disappointed.

But here we stand . . .

. . . His followers . . .

. . . blending in with the crowd.

Is this really where we were meant to be, standing with the crowd and looking just like everyone else? Can you tell the people of God from the rest? There's no use mincing words. We wear these masks for a reason. The biggest reason, if we're honest, is our own sin. Sin that's no different from that of those who've never found God.

According to several surveys, Christian people are divorcing at a pace that rivals their non-Christian friends. One study even said that 27 percent of born-again Christians are or have previously been divorced compared to 24 percent of all married couples.[2]

While 42 percent of Christian teens report having sexual intercourse by the age of eighteen, only a slightly higher 48 percent of their unchurched peers report the same.[3] And it seems to me that oral sex among Christian teens is possibly rivaling that of their unchurched peers, which is at about 50 percent.

It is estimated that one in four women has had an abortion. Thirty-three percent of born-again believers say abortion is acceptable. Forty-three percent of unbelievers agree.[4] Shouldn't there be a bigger difference between believers and the rest of the crowd?

Lying doesn't seem to slow down among regular church attendees, either. Sixty-seven percent of mainline Christian church attendees who said they tithed in the past year did not.[5]

Sixty-four percent of Christian men admit to struggling with a sexual addiction or compulsion, which might include Internet pornography, compulsive masturbation, or other secret sexual activity. Even four of every ten pastors report having used porn in the past year.[6]

We go to the same movies as everyone else. We watch the same TV. We invest in the same stuff. And we struggle with the same emotionally depleted hearts. We take the same antidepressants.

Ugh! Can you tell the people of God from the rest?

The apostle Paul once wrote, "[Let] there be no going along with the crowd, the empty-headed, mindless crowd. They've refused for so long to deal with God that they've lost touch not only with God but with reality itself." (That's *The Message* paraphrase of Ephesians 4:17–18. Sometimes I just love the simplicity with which it communicates.) Paul is seriously concerned with the fact that, in some cases, he can't tell the Christians in Ephesus from the rest of the bunch. All this blending resulted in spiritual eyes that were darkened to the understanding of the faith and power God meant for them to know. They no longer had a sense of reality but were living in a paradigm that was far from truth.

You *will not* find the way out in conventional wisdom. Nope! The Bible says that the great, exciting, blessed riches of God are *unsearchable* (Eph. 3:8–9). That doesn't mean you *can't* find it. The Greek word *anexichniaston*—don't ask me to say that—is what ends up in our Bibles as *unsearchable*. It meant "that which cannot be traced by human footprints." So stick with the crowd if you want, but I think you'll find those human footprints won't lead you to the great, exciting, blessed riches of the abundant life God has planned for you. To find that, you've got to follow the sovereign footprints of God.

The apostle Paul has some advice for us. It's written in the form of a prayer. In Ephesians 1:18 he writes, "I pray also that the eyes of your heart may be enlightened in order that you may know the hope to which he has called you, the riches of his glorious inheritance." My friend, remember we're not tracing something that human eyes can see. We've got to look with the eyes of our hearts. Eyes that only God can supernaturally open.

> *"Every human being on earth—*
> *whether he admits it or not—*
> *carries in his soul a dream,*
> *a sense of destiny, a longing for something greater*
> *than himself. God is the Dream Giver,*
> *and only He*
> *can fulfill your deepest desire."*[7]
> —BRUCE WILKINSON

IT'S TIME TO RE-DREAM

When I was twenty-five, I found myself so exhausted from the quest for a big bank account and titles of honor and success that I was mentally and physically unable to keep going. Already, my husband and I owned two radio stations, a marketing agency, and a monthly magazine in a small Midwestern town. I was standing in the middle of my dreams, and I felt completely unfulfilled. Depression was the nasty side effect of my workaholism. It was also the only consequence that could've gotten me to stop following the crowd in vain pursuits. I went to bed for several weeks, waking just to get everyone out the door and then to greet them and feed them in the afternoon. And, oh my, in all that quiet I saw more ugly and nasty sin.

I came to realize that I was using work and success to soothe a broken heart, a heart bloodied by terrible, deep, dark sin and heartache—the sexual sin from my teen years and a terribly wounded and off-course marriage. The worst part of it was that in the midst of my brokenness, I was a liar. I never told my husband I was a virgin when we married. I just carefully avoided telling him that I wasn't. I lied to my friends, always pretending that my marriage was picture-perfect. I had forgotten that God hates lies. My life was one great big lie. Masks breed lies like stagnant water breeds mosquitoes.

Do you feel a twinge of discomfort? Don't be discouraged. Discomfort right about now is a good thing. It is evidence of a heart that can feel the Holy Spirit's sweet nudge toward righteousness. If you feel discomfort about fitting in with the world, confess it and get excited about what comes next.

Bruce Wilkinson on the Dream Giver

When I first heard the name Bruce Wilkinson, it was in conjunction with his book *The Prayer of Jabez*. The next thing I knew he was a household name. It seemed he was set to be a comfortable Christian celebrity, when suddenly . . . what was this? He was moving to Africa? Why? For what? Didn't he know he was about to be set for life?

Bruce followed God's dream. I can promise you that there is nothing glamorous about living in Africa. God placed in Bruce's heart a dream that's enormous, even for an American household name with a *New York Times* best seller under his belt. He's been called to plant tens of thousands of Never Ending Gardens to feed the hungry in Africa. He's building African Dream Villages for orphans, tens of thousands at a shot. And he's fighting the pandemic of HIV/AIDS with his "Beat the Drum" teams. Each and every one of these projects requires his total dependence on God as he needs thousands of acres and dozens of volunteers who will leave the comfort of their own homelands to minister. I find myself wondering, if God gave me the potential of comfort here in America by giving me a bestseller, would I give it up to follow His dream? Certainly, Bruce is a man whose wisdom we can follow.

From his personal experience, Bruce promises this about our precious God: "The further you walk with Him, the more He will ask of you. More of your money, more of your service, more of your time. He'll even ask you to give Him your big dream. Until all that's left is one person—Jesus Christ. One day you'll awaken to the fact that you've chosen Him as your supreme purpose in life, and you'll realize that He Himself has been your greatest dream, your longing, your desperate desire all along."[8]

Remember those followers of Christ blending in with the crowd at the cross? Have you heard what those physically and emotionally depleted followers would soon begin to accomplish? They dove headfirst into the power of God.

Now, no doubt they had to look at things differently. The dream they'd had for an earthly kingdom had just been nailed to a cross. But God had a dream. The Spirit was about to come upon them to revive them and to fill them with a different dream.

A bigger dream.

A better dream.

A dream that had power they couldn't have imagined.

And through them . . . God has changed the world!

They had to be willing to do things God's way, not their own. They had to forfeit their hopes for an earthly kingdom—for power in the here and now—in order to embrace God's dream. They had to re-dream.

When I was a girl, I dreamed of being a missionary. When I grew up, I decided to be a raving success in the corporate world so that I could fund those serving God . . . since I myself felt unfit. I was pretty obsessed with my passion for success in the corporate arena. It was a dream I had to let die, and dreams like that don't die quickly or easily. I never *ever* dreamed of ministering to teens on the subject of sexual purity. I mean, if you'd have asked me about that just a few years ago, I'd have laughed. I had clearly told God that this closet of my heart wasn't to be opened to anyone but Him. He had a different idea.

I hesitated at every single step of the journey, pleading with God for something safer and less revealing. Let me say with certainty that the first year or so was a slow healing process. Each confession I made was painful and frightening. I simply had to be willing to do things God's way. My dreams were out the door! Taking my mask off meant living an entirely different life than I'd planned. I want to be the first to say this . . .

It's a bigger dream.

It's a better dream.

It's a dream I could not have imagined!

I had to re-dream.

My friend, are you ready to let God redirect you? Do you think you can embrace a bigger, better dream knowing it might mean forfeiting dreams you now cling to? It will probably mean making hard changes so you no longer blend in with the crowd. There will be moments when you think you can't bear it, but I assure you that we can work through most of the pain in the pages of this little book. Together we'll laugh at ourselves, and we may even have a little cry as we let go of the dreams we're clinging to so tightly. Will you stick with me?

Taking your mask off will absolutely require you to do things God's way. It'll just end up being a bigger mess if you don't. We must allow Him to open our spiritual eyes so that we can follow His footprints to find a revived life. Are you willing to let Him re-dream your life for you?

Before you really answer that question, you should probably peek at the next little thing you need to prepare for. Brace yourself!

⌒— It's Your Turn —⌒

Grab your journal and your Bible and open to Psalm 25.

Remember, our key verse is Psalm 25:14. In the King James Version, it reads, "The secret of the LORD is with them that fear him; and he will shew them his covenant." Look this passage up in your own Bible. Back up just a few verses. Read verses 4–9 (NIV). Just *before* the psalmist gets to our treasured verse, he demonstrates his willingness to follow God's plan rather than his own.

"Show me your ways, O LORD . . ."

"Teach me . . ."

"Guide me . . ."

"He guides the humble in what is right and teaches them *his* way."

Verse 8 is particularly comforting for those of us who feel overwhelmed by sin. It reads, "Good and upright is the LORD; therefore he instructs sinners in his ways." Does he instruct the perfect, masked pew sitters? He instructs sinners. That's me for sure! How about you?

It is vital that you get this going in. Discovering the secret of the Lord demands that you relinquish your plans and dreams, listen to His instructions, and walk in His dreams for you. Are you willing?

In your journal rewrite Psalm 25:4–9, and intimately talk to God about the unmet dream of your life. Was it to find the perfect man and settle down with a family? Was it to have a great career, but those three rapid pregnancies after you got married slowed you down? Was it to have children, but that's just not happening?

Is it possible that God wants you to be willing to follow another path? What might that be? Are you willing to pursue His dream for your life in order to find a place of friendship beyond your wildest dreams and to live *in* an amazing story of faith?

CHAPTER TWO

Prepare to Awaken the Enemy

See how my enemies have increased and how fiercely
they hate me! Guard my life and rescue me;
let me not be put to shame, for I take refuge in you.

—PSALM 25:19–20

ord," I prayed, as I snuggled into my cozy bed. "Please show me
what I need to do to bring these girls to You."

I lay there praying for the handful of girls at this little slumber
party, as I looked out into the forest. The room I was in had many
glass walls and large windows. It was as if I was sleeping in the great
outdoors.

I began to drift off, when suddenly I was inexplicably engulfed in
total fear. I reasoned with myself. "Dannah," I said, "you little chick-
en! You've always been afraid of the dark. Deal with it! Go to sleep."
Suddenly the openness of the room made me feel terribly unsafe. Was
I being watched? My mind began to race to wild conclusions.

The fear would not subside, so I began to pray. I prayed for all the
girls upstairs one by one.

17

"Dannah," a voice whispered. I jumped.

"Yes," I answered, seeing a girl poke her head into my room.

"Can I have the matches you used earlier tonight to light our candles?" she asked.

"Well, sure," I answered. "But why?"

"Oh," she responded without skipping a beat. "We just want to light some candles and have girl talk."

I handed her the matches and went quickly back to my praying, as my fear seemed to be escalating. I prayed, not knowing what on earth was wrong with me. Maybe it was because I was feeling inadequate. Maybe these girls just weren't going to respond.

"Lord," I cried. "Help!"

Then, just as suddenly as the fear came, it left, leaving peace. I crawled back into bed and fell asleep within moments.

One week later . . .

Jordon's mom walked toward me on the open sidewalk, with a determined look on her face. "Hey, Jordon loved the retreat last weekend!" she said. "I've been dying to tell you this really cool thing that happened in her life."

I was eager to hear what it was. "Tell me," I said.

"After you went to bed, some of the girls decided to have a séance," the mother told me.

She had my attention!

"Well, Jordon just sat on her bed scared to death, knowing it was wrong," this mother reported. "As you know, she's very shy . . . not a confronter. She didn't know what to do and was kind of waiting for someone else to stop the whole thing. About then, one of the girls came *downstairs to ask you for matches or something. Jordon just prayed and prayed, but nothing happened to stop it. The girls configured in some special circle and began to light candles in the middle.*

"Suddenly, Jordon just stood up and said, 'NO! You have no idea what power you're playing with. I'm not going to do this! I'm going to have a prayer circle over here on my bed, and anyone who wants to join me is welcome.' One by one the girls joined Jordon. They never did have a séance."

Hmmmm, *I thought to myself.* So that's what all that fear was about.

Let me be very blunt. Heaven and hell are slugging it out over you. Yes, you!

God knows your name. So does Satan.

This might be a frightening thought, but there's no middle ground. In the Bible, many of the letters written to churches such as those in Ephesus and Galatia contain warnings about Satan's desire to engulf them. Why do these books written to believers come filled with information on spiritual warfare? I believe it is because Satan works feverishly to keep us from living in the secret of the Lord—being an intimate part of God's family, experiencing His reviving power. (As we move along in our understanding of the secret of the Lord, you'll see just how powerful it can be. We're almost there. In the next chapter, we'll launch our deep exploration of Psalm 25:14.)

SATAN'S RESPONSE TO INTIMACY

I believe Satan hates intimacy in the body of Christ. He wants to decimate the intimate sense of belonging that God created for the body. He wants to keep you locked in a place of isolation. Why? You're not much of a threat to him there. You won't do much with a faith that's merely a routine and steady observance. You'll just experience church much as you would a country club. It's going to simply be a place you go to socialize with people who have similar interests, beliefs, and families. That's *not* really church! So, he'll leave you alone.

But step into where we're headed and he will take note of you. I really wasn't prepared for that. I'd been a Christian for two decades of my life and seen little evidence with my own two eyes to prove a supernatural battle. I thought all that demonic stuff was relegated to third world countries with voodoo dolls and witch doctors. I could believe it was possible in *those* places, but certainly it wasn't possible in our sophisticated "Christian" country to encounter the demonic realm! I was wrong. The moment you step into the power of the secret of the Lord, you will hit Satan's radar screen.

Looking back, I think I first hit it when I was fifteen. Please understand that I take full responsibility for my sexual sin. At the same time, it was unbelievably out of character with the rest of my life and my intense love for Jesus. I was absolutely blindsided by temptation. How did it happen? Satan turned up the heat when I started to experience an intimate and powerful faith. I was none the wiser, so I fell, and hard.

The second time around, I *was* wiser. When he showed up again, I ran as fast as I could into the arms of Jesus. I was very aware of what was happening. I'd awakened the enemy.

Satan in Peer Countries: A Blatant Presence

Perhaps it will be easier to believe if we look at a country more like our own in terms of technology and intellect. Let's look at China. It is a sophisticated first world country. Though the country is Communist, the kingdom of God is growing rapidly there. These believers have discovered the secret of the Lord in a very profound way. The government permits Chinese believers to join a state-appointed "Christian" organization so that they can worship "freely," but in doing so, Chinese believers must agree to turn their backs on certain foundational doctrines, books of the Bible, and Christian practices, including evangelism. In short, you can call yourself a Christian as long as you just don't "be" one. In this way, the government of China is able to boast that it no longer persecutes Christians. Nothing could be further from the truth.

Most Chinese believers meet in illegal house churches. The movement began in the 1970s. In the early '90s it was so powerful that it was estimated that 22,000 people were coming to Christ *daily!*[1] Every January since 1994, the organized network of secret house churches has "Gospel Month," in which each believer may choose to risk his or her freedom, and perhaps life, by sharing his or her testimony of salvation with three unbelievers. In the first year, 13,000 new believers were baptized as a result. The next year, 123,000 were baptized![2]

Liu Zhenying, known as Brother Yun, has been one of the courageous leaders of this house church network. He's endured beatings, separation from his family, three significant prison sentences for expressing his faith, and horrible forms of torture, including electric batons and needles inserted between his fingernails and flesh. Don't forget, this country is every bit the intellectual, political, and technological peer of Western first world countries.

During one of his prison terms, Brother Yun's wife, Deling, forgot the battle that she was in . . . the battle between heaven and hell. She convinced herself that she needed sleep more than she needed to pray. She decided to ask God to allow her to fellowship with Him in her sleep. She invited Him to speak to her spirit as she rested. She got quite a wake-up call one night when she lay down to sleep.

Isaac and I were just falling asleep when I saw a dark demonic figure standing at the foot of my bed. I was terrified.

I started to pray loudly and fervently. I shouted, "In the name of Jesus I fight against you, Satan. I stand against all your lies. You have deceived me into thinking I can pray in my sleep. I bind you in Jesus' name!"

I felt a demonic presence brush past me as I prayed these words. A tiny bell was attached to the end of my leather belt, which was hanging on the end of the bed. The bell started ringing by itself. I understood immediately that the devil wanted to distract me by this ringing, so I ignored it and continued praying. Soon the demonic presence left and a deep peace came upon us.

Yun's mother was walking home at that same time. When she was still about one mile from our village she heard what she thought were dozens of Christians praying loudly, so she ran home to join the prayer meeting. When she arrived she was amazed to find that it was only me who had been praying.[3]

> *"We have always been disposed to believe what the Bible says about the spiritual world, even when it seems to conflict with the Western worldview . . . Ministries that ignore the reality of the spiritual world don't have an adequate answer, but neither do some deliverance ministries that see the problem as only spiritual."*[4]
>
> —NEIL T. ANDERSON AND DAVE PARK

Why do I tell you this? Because I truly believe the power of the secret of the Lord to be so threatening to Satan that he'll lock you into his radar as you begin to discover it. The story I shared at the beginning of the chapter was my first awareness of the enemy. I've had many others since then, some far more threatening, but not one of them fruitful on the enemy's behalf. Every single one of them has been a faith builder for me . . . providing more stories of God's power and miracles!

Sometimes, the way that the enemy attacks doesn't appear in the form of dark figures or ringing bells on bedposts. Sometimes he comes in subtly so that we don't recognize him.

SATAN IN THE WESTERN WORLD: A SUBTLE PRESENCE

When I first took off my mask with Bob, I felt such relief. However, as my healing occurred, God sometimes asked me to share my story, sometimes one-on-one and other times in small groups. Each time, the days and weeks that followed were emotionally excruciating. I felt so foolish. In my heart, I believed my testimony had discredited God. I had a heavy sense of oppression and fear. I cried a lot.

That, my friend, is the enemy working. When you share God's loving rescue from your sin, you honor Him. It says so in Psalm 50. Verses 9–10, 12 read: "I have no need of a bull from your stall or of goats from your pens, for every animal of the forest is mine, and the cattle on a thousand hills . . . If I were hungry I would not tell you, for the world is mine, and all that is in it." This made me wonder: *What can we bring to the table to serve God? Does God have a way for us to be of use to Him?* Verse 15 concisely says, "I will deliver you, and you will honor me."

Our stories of God's deliverance and rescue from sin are the place of God's honor. Satan will make us think they should be kept silent. What a lie!

How did I overcome this attack? I used 2 Timothy 1:7. The New King James Version says, "For God has not given us a spirit of fear, but of power and of love and of a sound mind." Right now, if you feel "afraid" of who might know about your past sin, you're being lied to. That's not from God.

OPPRESSION OR DEPRESSION?

One of Satan's favorite subtle persecutions is oppression.

Ten years ago, I was *de*pressed. I was emotionally and physically depleted. As a result, my body was sorely lacking in serotonin. Working thirteen-hour days had taken its toll. I got some good Christian counseling and mentoring, prayed fervently, and took a six-month course of a common antidepressant. I came out on the other side emotionally strong again.

Three years ago, I was "at the top of my game." My life was in balance as I worked and played with my family. No more thirteen-hour days! I felt great. Suddenly, a terrible family crisis occurred. Overnight, I returned to symptoms similar to what I'd experienced when I was *de*pressed, including not eating. I told my mom I was going to see the doctor. She stopped me. "Have you considered that this could be spiritual and *not* physical?" she asked. She encouraged me to pray first.

My friend Janet was called by the Lord to pray with me. Our prayers were simple but fervent. At about 1:00 in the morning it broke. I actually felt a lifting that I cannot explain. I stood up and giggled and said, "I'm starved. Anyone want a late night bowl of cereal?" I hadn't been *de*pressed. I was *op*pressed.

I believe both are possible. Neil T. Anderson, author of *The Bondage Breaker*, encourages us not to polarize to either extreme. Rather, we should treat emotional problems both physically and spiritually. He says that "there is no inner conflict which is not psychological, because there is never a time when your mind, emotions and will are not involved. Similarly, there is no problem which is not spiritual. There is no time when God is not present or when it is safe for you to take off the armor of God."[5] His book is an excellent tool for you if you have been struggling with emotional issues.

When I was overwhelmed with this fear, I'd pray the verse out loud. "Oh God, I know You haven't given me a spirit of fear, so this is not from You. I reject it. Instead, I ask You to fill me with power, a sense that I am loved and can pour out love, and give me a mind that is at peace!" At first, this was a sheer act of obedience, since God's Word tells us that the Word of God is our weapon against Satan. However, I soon found that those attacks came less and less often. For some time they didn't occur at all. They do still occur infrequently, usually when I'm just about to break through into some new territory for God. When they do, I fight them in this same way.

I assume that since you're still here with me, you're willing to allow God to redirect your life. Now, are you ready to enter into the battle of the universe?

If so, let's begin to explore the secret of the Lord more deeply.

⌀— It's Your Turn —⌀

I'd like you to pause right now and read Psalm 25. I want you to get a broad overview of the whole chapter before we dive into our special verse.

(No cheating! Get your Bible out, girl! And come right back.)

Remember, our key verse is 14 (and it may sound different in your version). The writer has knowledge of the secret of the Lord to be able to write about it. Now, check out what follows that treasured verse in verses 19 and 20. They read, "See how my enemies have increased and how fiercely they hate me! Guard my life and rescue me; let me not be put to shame, for I take refuge in you." The writer notes the escalating furor of the enemy.

You simply must be ready for that.

Perhaps you already see the enemy at work. Won't you just take a moment and ask for God's protection? Write a prayer in your journal to that effect.

PART TWO

The Secret of the Lord

CHAPTER THREE

A Prescription for Loneliness

Turn to me and be gracious to me,
for I am lonely and afflicted.
—PSALM 25:16

*D*on't do it," something inside of me whispered. "They'll never understand. It'll just discredit your ministry to teen girls."

There was an intense warring in my spirit.

I'd decided that tonight was the night. I needed to tell some friends about my secret shame. We were in Cathy's bedroom, escaping the husbands and babies for a few moments of girl talk. I couldn't have imagined its being this perfect. Had God orchestrated this privacy? If so, why on earth did I feel this sudden urge to keep my mouth shut?

I watched the other three talking and laughing as if I wasn't even there. Which of these voices was God? Which was not?

"I . . . uh . . ." I tried to interrupt. What was this? Tears? No! Oh, I didn't want this to be a big deal.

The others went suddenly quiet. There was no backing out now.

"Well . . . I think God told me to tell you something," I blurted out, glancing at Donna, my dear friend from college . . . Christian college. What was she going to think of me? Why was my fear of what she'd think so much more intense than what I felt about the other two?

"It's an old sin . . . a secret," I started and stopped. "Took me three hours to tell Bob . . . bet the guys won't watch the babies that long."

We laughed that crazy girl laugh that only comes in the middle of tears.

"It happened when I was fifteen," I said. "I didn't think it'd be something I could ever do . . . don't even know the guy anymore . . . yeah, OK . . . that's all."

Silence.

Awkward stillness.

And then, a sweet embrace.

A new flood of healing.

I think I knew now which voice was telling me to just let it out. Only God could bring such warmth to a person's inner being.

Have you ever been lonely?

I have.

What is loneliness? Ironically it's not necessarily being alone. Although you may experience the kind of loneliness that comes from the absence of people, there is another form of loneliness. The strange thing about this loneliness is that we feel it most intensely when we are with people. Loneliness is the knowing in our hearts that we were created to really, truly know each other in the deepest sense, but we feel stuck with superficiality. Sometimes we're stuck with moments of superficiality, causing brief brushes with loneliness. Sometimes we're stuck with a life overwhelmingly flavored with loneliness as we hide sins . . . or, worse yet, bare them and find those we pour our hearts out to incapable of talking about real things.

In my case, past sin kept me lonely for many years. But it's not always sin that keeps us lonely. Sometimes it's just great painful points in our lives that invite loneliness to blanket us. It comes in many forms and it comes to many.

RECOGNIZING LONELINESS

Loneliness is talking about cake icing when your husband just lost his job because he's been viewing porn at work.

Loneliness is putting on a happy face for the big family Christmas party even though your child battles cancer.

Loneliness is laughing with friends about last night's must-see-TV even though your mind is on your parents' divorce.

Loneliness is going to another bridal shower and never talking about the loss of the guy you thought was "the one."

Loneliness is gathering in the cul-de-sac to talk about the weather when you'd rather talk about your financial fears.

It's most often triggered by a major painful event such as the divorce of parents, a major dating breakup, an illness or a long hospitalization, the loss of a loved one, a broken friendship, your own divorce, the loss of a job, the death of a dream, rejection from a group of people you trusted, or a battle with sin.

> *"Americans are among*
> *the loneliest people in the world."*[1]
>
> —GEORGE GALLUP, JR.

Just yesterday I picked up my *Christianity Today* to read about the very lovely and world-impacting Joni Eareckson Tada. She's a powerful presence despite her quadriplegia. She started her graceful ministry years ago by drawing intricate pictures with her mouth, since her hands have no sensation or strength. She has gone on to be a valiant voice for God, tackling issues as simple as getting wheelchairs to the poor or as challenging as stem-cell research. Today she's a hero to many, disabled and able-bodied alike. But she knows loneliness.

> I struggle with loneliness when we go to a friend's house for dinner. Last night we went to a friend's house and the whole party has to stop because Joni is here. Let's go outside and see Ken unfold the ramp. Isn't that great? Where'd you get that ramp? . . . Dinner's ready and I can't go into the kitchen to help with the hors d'oeuvres or get the drinks. I'm a clumsy roadblock to everyone in the kitchen. And I don't often fit, watching ESPN with the guys.
>
> I feel lonely when people look at me and I can't talk to them because they must tell me what an inspiration I am, and oh I read your book, and oh I love you and you're so great. I just want to talk to people.[2]

It's the high-visibility leaders who are struggling with loneliness. It's also the nameless faces sitting next to you. Read what one precious young woman wrote to me recently:

> I've had five major brain surgeries in the past four years and I'm not anything like the "Homecoming queen, head cheerleader, top-of-the-class, had so many friends I couldn't count them, kept on going like the energizer bunny" person I used to be . . . It seems now that all my old friends are living out my crushed dreams. They're married, in college, have full-time jobs . . . and have no time to do anything with me . . . I know they love me; but it's killing me. Everywhere I go people run up to me and tell me how good I look and ask how I'm doing. I'm like a celebrity in my town . . . Though their love means sooo much to my family and I hold "superficially happy" conversations with everyone, I'm still just sooo lonely.

The body of Christ is lonely. We all experience it at some point in our lives. It's not a sin. (According to John 16:32, Jesus knew acute loneliness.) But it's not something with which God wants you to live. So, how do you relieve loneliness? That, my friend, is where we begin to deepen our understanding of the secret of the Lord.

You see, loneliness is really the opposite of "the secret of the Lord." As I shared earlier, this is a rich Hebrew phrase that speaks of the intimate friendship that exists between believers. It speaks of a tight-knit group with unconditional trust; a circle of friends among whom weaknesses, strengths, successes, and failures are shared. Even sins are confessed openly. When we become intimate, we become a part of the secret. Together, we *are* the secret. No masks of perfection here. We are truly known.

Here's where we find the great crisis. The fellowship you have with other believers is *meant* to be mask free. Instead, we often wear our best masks to appear perfect when we head to church. We sit in the pews, thinking ourselves to be the only one struggling with our particular pain. We're lonely.

We must all dive in to become the secret of the Lord—so tight-knit that we talk about real things in real time in total truth . . . no matter how ugly they might be. That means we take off the mask and become transparent, so intimacy can grow, and our friendships are rooted so deep that they aid us in our times of deepest need.

How do we get into the precious secret of the Lord? That's easy . . . or I should say it's easily explained. My friend, you have to take off your mask!

Taking Off Your Mask

Who knows your darkest secrets . . . you know, the ones Satan uses to tell you that you aren't fit for a big plan . . . can't possibly have a special purpose with *that* in your life? You wouldn't believe how much those lies about your inferiority would be crushed if you'd just reach out and tell an older, wiser, godly person about your shame. James 5:16 says, "Confess your sins to each other and pray for each other so that you may be healed." Tell someone. You'll be healed from the loneliness, healed from the shame, and healed from the grief.

Now, I don't want to drag up old junk that God's already dealt with. That's simply not necessary. I'm not asking you to share that stuff. I'm talking about that one subject that comes up and—wham!—you immediately feel all alone in your shame. Who sees behind that mask of yours? Who is helping you get past the hurt that's holding you back? Who's cheering for you to achieve your most heartfelt dreams? Those dreams you've had since you were a child, but . . . well, then you grew up and "realized how foolish they were" or "how disqualified you have become." Maybe you just need someone to speak confidence into you so you can re-dream yourself right into God's amazing plan for your life.

If you want healing from loneliness, you've got to take off that mask, my friend. I know you feel as though you'll face unbearable rejection. That's simply not how it works in most cases.

Recently, the most amazing thing happened in my congregation. A few teens were baptized. The last one we'll call Traci. Before she was baptized, she explained that she'd struggled with drugs, sex, and depression, and that just a few weeks earlier she'd attempted suicide. She humbly confessed her sin and her need for ongoing discipleship to overcome it. Then she went down. And so did we.

I didn't understand it completely at first. Tears flowed. Hearts repented. All over the room there were little circles of prayer and confession suddenly taking place. A pastor confessed to needing accountability to overcome pornography. And though names were not shared, I heard of broken marriages being mended and of others who were in confusing, painful places of sin finding hope. There is no telling what else happened that day; these are just the stories I know about. It wasn't planned. And while it wasn't remotely organized, it wasn't chaotic. It was holy. There was no sermon that day.

I later learned that two weeks before the youth group was to leave for a missions trip, someone dropped out. Our youth pastor, Keith, consulted our head pastor, Paul.

"I'd like to just blow someone away," Keith said. "I want to invite someone who maybe would never expect it."

"How about Traci?" Paul suggested.

I can only imagine the look on Keith's face. I bet it said, "You mean the girl who overdosed on heroin two months ago?" Keith admits that he had to pray about it, but after one night, he was able to make contact with Traci. Even stranger, just three days before the youth group was scheduled to leave, Traci had a meltdown and attempted suicide. Pastor Keith and the others prayed and felt God saying that she should still go. Of course, Keith had to convince the medical authorities that it would be a good decision to let Traci out of her suicide watch two days early in order to make this trip. They eventually agreed to release her . . . nine hours before the youth group departed for Jamaica. And on that little island, Traci met God in a new way. The youth group loved her, accepted her, and opened up and was transparent because of her. It didn't just change her. It changed many of them. And that changed many of the adults in our church who'd been stuck behind masks for years. That's what the secret of the Lord does. It changes all of us.

Now, don't run out and remove your mask just yet. I want to offer you some ideas on how to proceed, so stick with me for a few chapters as we explore this first phrase of our key verse. You'll be much better equipped to get that mask off with minimal pain.

RELEASING GOD'S POWER

As our relationships are made into what they are meant to be, God's power is released. What a motivator for Satan to keep us isolated.

For ten years, I was lonely because of sin even though I was mentally aware that God had forgiven me. I really needed to know that I was not alone, but the enemy convinced me that I was. I was sure I was the only Christian girl to sin like *that*. That was a lie. It held me back from healing, which in turn gagged me from speaking my testimony and helping others find healing.

Speaking of which, I often see three common lies that women who are lonely can't seem to break through. I'm ready to see us overcome them; are you? Friend, let's bust down some lies of hell! Follow me as we explore the first lie. Have you ever heard this whispered into your head? "I'm all alone here!"

ARE YOU LONELY?

Are you lonely? Here's how you might be able to tell. Answer yes or no to all of these questions.

1. Has there been a significant painful event in your life in the past twelve months? (Parents' divorce, loss of a job, hospitalization, etc.)

2. Do you zone out when people start talking about superficial things, desiring to talk about "real" issues? (Perhaps you avoid or leave parties.)

3. Do you feel painfully isolated when you are with people? (If being alone is comfortable for you, but being with people

makes you feel alone, you are probably experiencing this kind of loneliness.)

4. Do you cry often and feel sadness, but still maintain productivity and efficiency? (Depression dampens ability to function. Loneliness does not. If you find yourself unable to perform, you should consider the possibility that you may be suffering from depression, which can occur if loneliness goes on too long.)

5. Do you have a shameful issue that your spouse does not know about (perhaps a moment of unfaithfulness, a past abortion, or a friend of the opposite sex)?

6. Do you have a vibrant faith, but have a husband who does not believe in Christ as his Savior?

7. Do you have a shameful issue that your best friend or close friends do not know about? (Perhaps your husband has been using pornography, you're experiencing embarrassing financial problems, or you have lost a child that no one knows about.)

8. Do you feel that the only person you can really talk to is someone you pay, like a counselor or therapist?

If you answered yes to any of the above, you may be experiencing loneliness on some level.

‿ It's Your Turn ‿

Presenting Your Loneliness to God

In Psalm 25, David cries out, "I am lonely and afflicted" (v. 16). His quest for the secret of the Lord was prompted by loneliness. Loneliness often seems to be the impetus for us today to find that place of reviving intimacy. If you have even a twinge of loneliness, I want you to follow David's example. Pour it out to God. In your journal, just lay it out word by word, tear by tear. This is the beginning of finding the secret.

CHAPTER FOUR

Lie #1: "I'm All Alone Here!"

*Remember not the sins of my youth and my rebellious
ways; according to your love remember me,
for you are good, O LORD.*

—PSALM 25:7

Rrrrring.

"Hello," I answered.

"Dannah," a voice whispered. I stood taller, alerted to the need I sensed on the other end of the phone line.

"Yes," I said, trying to identify the familiar voice.

Quiet.

"This is . . ." The frightened voice cracked as she said her name.

"Are you OK?" I asked. "Do you need me to do something?"

Dead silence.

"I . . . ah," she labored. "I just needed to tell you . . ." Tears interrupted her.

"I'm coming over," I said.

"No . . . no . . . wait," she cried. "I have to say this."

I waited. Just last night I vaguely mentioned to this new friend that I had a sin in my past that had left a deep scar. I was hoping she was a safe place. As I listened to her talk, my mind immediately began to assume that she too had committed sexual sin and needed me as much as I needed her.

"I had one too!" she finally blurted.

I realized then that something wasn't going quite right. She was going out on a limb with something and thought I would be there with her. I was pretty sure I wasn't. I needed to move tenderly.

"Had one what?" I gently nudged.

"An abortion . . . it happened when I was in high school. My boyfriend never knew my parents made me. It wasn't my choice. I think about it every day . . ." she motored on as the confession rolled out of her like a great ocean wave. I listened quietly.

"Have you ever told anyone?" I asked, but knowing all too well the answer.

"No!" she gasped as if she couldn't believe I'd asked.

"Does your husband know?" I asked.

"Of course not. I could never tell him," she told me. "Until you confessed it last night, I thought there would never be anyone I could talk to about it, ever. You don't know what this means to me."

"I do know what this means to you," I said, dreading what I was about to tell her. "I'm in a lot of ways in the same place you are. Until very, very recently I'd never told anyone about my sin. It's the most frightening thing on earth."

I realized then how terribly awkward my confession to her had been and that I'd obviously left a lot open to interpretation.

"I need to tell you something, though," I said. "This doesn't at all

change the fact that we can really help each other through this, OK? I did not have an abortion. I did have a sexual relationship when I was fifteen. It still hurts very much. I think we should get together and talk. What do you think?"

Quiet on the phone line. I could feel her recoiling.

"Dannah, I never called you," she said with certainty. "We can never talk about this!"

The phone line went dead.

So did the relationship, try as I might to warm it. I mean, we were friendly and shared recipes, but something in the relationship died that day.

She slipped her mask back on as tightly as ever. As long as I knew her, she never took it off.

Last week, my sweet tweenage daughter, Lexi, decided it was time to rearrange her room. So, she gutted every drawer, corner, and nook and cranny. I'll commend her for the ambition of her idea, but the result . . . well, let's just say there was still much potential (to put it kindly). She'd made the mess, but each day she'd plead with me to help her. I did a few times. (Yep, the mess was that big!) Finally, it was manageable and I wanted her to tackle it on her own. I gently prodded her each day to spend a little time in there making it just a little better. She didn't, and she became increasingly frustrated with the mess. Finally, I told her she could spend time with friends only after the room was clean. She looked at me astonished, realizing she was on her own. "But what do you want *me* to do?" she asked in shock. I actually laughed. It was so obvious. (This wasn't rocket science.)

At that moment, I felt God chuckling, too.

"That's you sometimes, Dannah," He said, "always shocked when I point out the clutter and junk in your life."

Sometimes we're like that. We just want God to be this butler that we order around to clean up our lives. We become like indignant children when nothing changes. All the while, it's quite obvious to God that what we need to do is roll up our sleeves and get rid of a few feet of the junk in our lives!

Before I began to live in the secret of the Lord, I had entire mountains of junk in my life. Debt. Busy-ness. Workaholism. Greed. Pride. Material passions. I was a believer who really wasn't living like one. At the same time, I really thought I was the poster child for Christian influence in my little business world! I was leading Bible studies in my circle of friends, albeit with few life-changing results in any of them. I was volunteering for VBS, nursery duty, and other simple tasks. I even joined a committed, small band of believers to dig deeply into our faith through an intense twelve-week study course. Still, I just wasn't very satisfied . . . didn't seem to have the power in my life that the Bible promises to us. It was something I couldn't reconcile with my faith. I wondered if I was the only one like this.

You Are Not Alone

You and I are not alone in our constant struggle to ward off sin and temptation and the fight against its lingering effects. Until we own that and stop parading around as if perfect, there will be very little power of God manifested in our lives. All too often, I meet women who are just about to break through and tell someone what they're struggling with, but they shut down. Why? They come to believe that they're the only one who's struggled with such a thing. That is one of the greatest lies of hell.

"Hold Me Jesus," a song by the late anointed musician and poet Rich Mullins, has almost a lullaby quality to it. To the soft cadence of piano and strings, Rich cries for the King of Heaven to hold him because he's literally shaking. He craves God's peace. The song is clean and comforting until you realize how terribly uncomfortable Rich was when he penned it. He once wrote about the song:

> I was in Amsterdam, and there was so much sin all around us. After years of behaving myself as best as I could, I was really having to hang on for dear life. I was thinking, "No one would know. I could do anything I wanted to do. Wouldn't it be fun to just cut loose for a couple nights and misbehave as much as I want?"[1]

Rich didn't cut loose. He cut to the chase with God in writing "Hold Me Jesus." I don't imagine it was a shopping spree or overeating that was tempting him. He's confessed to struggling with "alcohol and other addictions." The party atmosphere in the Amsterdam streets was calling to him in the night. I can just imagine the temptation that rattled him as he wrote this song, which brings so much comfort to me and many others.

You are not alone!

Even our most public, honored Christian leaders are prone to great temptation. Kay Arthur confesses that her suicidal tendency, which plagued her before she began her walk with Christ, returned once at the height of her ministry. Jack Hayford once shared with a crowd at a Promise Keepers gathering a vivid moment of sexual temptation. He did not succumb to it, but by the audience's response, he was speaking to many men who had.

You are not alone!

Sometimes our leaders don't say no to the onslaught of temptation. They fall. I think of Pastor Gordon MacDonald, whose adulterous affair led to the loss of his ministry when it was at its pinnacle and he had much national prominence. His is a story of the secret of the Lord. His congregation valiantly stepped up to love him through his period of painful repentance. Then, they put him right back into his place of leadership stronger than ever, where he remains today. And living a life of purity, too! It thrills my heart to see his name on Christianity Today's *Leadership Journal* as editor-at-large, or on the list of the board he chairs for World Relief. He has been fully restored! Yes! I could scream with delight! In fact, I think I will!

You are not alone!

The Secret of the Lord Is a Safe Place to Confess Sin

The secret of the Lord, remember, is a place that deals *openly* with sin. In Psalm 25:7, David writes, "Remember not the sins of my youth and my rebellious ways." No bones about it. This king openly sang about his sin in this published psalm. We have to actually see our need before we become part of the secret of the Lord. The membership requirement is simple. You've gotta be a sinner. I make it a practice to continually ask the Lord to reveal to me my sin so that I'm aware of it.

How painful it was a few years ago when He confronted me with a brand-new sin—one I hadn't seen before. Through the summer, the Lord kept prodding my heart about this certain struggle. My husband gently suggested that he'd noticed this area of weakness in me. But it wasn't until I read Nancy Leigh DeMoss's confession about the same sin in her book *Brokenness* that I was able to even begin to see that my life was being cluttered by some junk. Nancy wrote:

> When I was in my mid-twenties, God's Spirit began to convict me that I had developed a habit of "exaggerating the truth" in certain situations. ("Exaggeration" is actually a proud, unbroken word for "lying.") Driven to make a good impression on others, I was frequently guilty of "stretching" the truth. Though no one else knew of my deception, and though others might have considered my offenses relatively inconsequential, I experienced an almost suffocating (and blessed!) sense of God's conviction in my heart, and I knew this was something I had to bring into the light.
>
> I agreed with God, confessed my deception, and purposed to begin speaking the truth in every situation. But I soon discovered that lying was a stronghold in my life—it was deeply ingrained. I was hooked and couldn't seem to get set free. Ultimately, the freedom that I needed and longed for began when I was willing to let the walls down. God brought to mind the principle of James 5:16, "Confess your trespasses to one another, and pray for one another, that you may be healed."[2]

Nancy did confess her sin of lying to two godly friends and found the secret of the Lord—that place where transparency breaks Satan's blackmailing power. And she was set free of her stronghold.

As I read Nancy's confession, I finally began to consider that this sin might be in me, too. I asked God to show me through specific circumstances if He was saying that I needed to confess and overcome the sin of lying. Even at this point, I was pretty confident He'd give me a God-hug and tell me I was being ridiculous. (I wish!)

Shortly after that, I was sitting in my mom's house with my mom and my husband, Bob, and we began to talk about Lexi's clay sculpture, which she was entering in a local fair's art competition. (Can a mother get off track for just a moment to brag? She's an extremely talented artist, and she got a blue ribbon for that sculpture!)

"I just love that stuff," Bob chimed in. "I think we should decorate our whole house with stuff the kids have made out of clay."

"Really," my mom said, seeming to jump at the chance. "Do *I* have something for *you*!" She came back from the closet with . . . what was that? It seemed familiar, but why?

"Dannah made this clay pot for me when she was in seventh grade," she said proudly. "I'd love for you to add it to your collection at home."

There it was. The evidence.

I *was* a liar. I *didn't* make that pot. When I was in seventh grade, I'd stolen it from the shelves when mine didn't turn out. I'd brought it home for my mother's approval. And I'd gotten it. But not really. It was a big, fat lie. (Let me tell you, God answers prayer!)

When I found myself struggling with lying, I couldn't even

speak of it. Hadn't I been a Christian for nearly three decades? Hadn't I been serving God through teaching and writing? Pride, perhaps the greatest sin I continually struggle with, crept in to silence my conscience. But my dear husband wouldn't let my pride win. He kept lovingly nudging me. That's what happens when we're in the secret of the Lord. Those around us call us on the carpet when they see sin in our lives! Ephesians calls us to live a life worthy of the calling we've received in Christ and, when one of us isn't, we "speak the truth in love."

> *"There is a beautiful transparency*
> *to honest disciples who never wear a false face*
> *and do not pretend to be anything but*
> *who they are. . . . Getting honest with ourselves*
> *does not make us unacceptable to God.*
> *It does not distance us from God,*
> *but draws us to Him—as nothing else can—*
> *and opens us anew to the flow of grace."*[3]
>
> —BRENNAN MANNING

I was shakin' in my shoes, feeling like a seventh grader all over again. I knew that to be fully released from that sin, as well as to overcome my habit of lying, I needed to tell my mom. I sat there, trying to walk circles around the confession until I finally just said it outright.

"I didn't make that pot," I confessed. "I stole it because I loved your praise, and I just didn't seem to make pots quite like that one."

I waited. Would she be angry? Disappointed? It's so amazing how the enemy could make me feel so afraid even as a middle-aged woman.

"Well," said my mom. "I have a confession to make to you too. Of all the pots you ever brought home, I *never* liked that one. That's why I was trying to pawn it off to Bob!"

The irony of it. Our lies are never nearly as useful as the truth, are they?

Now, the clay pot was probably my worst lie. I'd actually stolen something and willfully lied. And it did not matter that it had happened years and years ago. It needed to be confessed and made right, if possible. But here I was, in my thirties, and I was still lying. It's not always that obvious, though. Sometimes we have "less offensive" forms of lying that we call equivocation or exaggeration. That's what I found to be the flavor of my conversation all too often.

God used that summer to slay me and, through accountability with Bob, confession to my mom, and a lot of prayer, I was able to begin to break the pattern. I have to emphasize that without the confession to my husband and my mother, I would not have been able to overcome this. It was also impossible for Nancy Leigh DeMoss to overcome it outside of the secret of the Lord. How grateful I am to her for helping me to see my sin and to know that I was not alone in it.

Philip Yancey once wrote a column on the lessons we, the church, can learn from Alcoholics Anonymous. In AA, the members are very aware that they are not alone. This gives them freedom to confess. It also gives them compassion to love those who are doing the confessing. The words of one long-standing attending member, who is also a Christian, ring in my mind.

> When I'm late to church, people turn around and stare at me with frowns of disapproval. I get the clear message that I'm not as responsible as they are. When I'm late to AA, the meeting comes to a halt and everyone jumps up to hug and welcome me. They realize that my lateness may be a sign that I almost didn't make it. When I show up, it proves that my desperate need for them won out over my desperate need for alcohol.[4]

I long for the day when Christians operate with the same compassion and intimacy as those who attend Alcoholics Anonymous. When the support in the body of Christ is a stronger force than the pull of our deepest sins, we will be the secret of the Lord.

Be honest. Are you up to your knees in junk? You are not alone!

WHAT'S YOUR ADDICTION?

We've been together for a while now, and I imagine you've discovered something that's plastering a mask to your face. But, if you haven't, search deeply. I've found that there's *always* an area of my life that God would like to clean up. What might be hindering you from experiencing intimacy with other believers? Is it lying? Food addiction? Work addiction? Praise addiction? Gossiping? It could be just about anything, and when you ask God to let your spiritual eyes see your sin, you may be surprised what becomes visible. Brennan Manning gives us some eye-opening counsel when he writes,

Honesty is such a precious commodity that it is seldom found in the world or the church. Honesty requires the truthfulness to admit attachment and addictions that control our attention, dominate our consciousness, and function as false gods. I can be addicted to vodka or to being nice, to marijuana or being loved, to cocaine or being right, to gambling or relationships, to golf or gossiping. Perhaps my addiction is food, performance, money, popularity, power, revenge, reading, television, tobacco, weight, or winning. When we give anything more priority than we give to God, we commit idolatry. Thus we all commit idolatry countless times every day.[5]

☙ — IT'S YOUR TURN — ❧

What junk in your life needs to be exposed to release God's potential in your life? Write a new confession to God in your journal. Begin by opening your Bible and meditating on Psalm 25:7. By meditate, I mean read it and then close your eyes and think on it, asking God to reveal to you a very specific truth through it. Rewrite it in your journal, specifically mentioning the sin that God brings to mind as you meditate.

Chapter Five

Lie #2: "There's No One I Can Talk To"

> *Many of those who believed now came*
> *and openly confessed their evil deeds.*
> —ACTS 19:18

How did I get here so fast?

It seemed like just yesterday that I was trying to figure out how to confess my sin for the first time. Now I found myself often sharing my "ministry" to teen girls with others I met.

"I love what you're doing," said a woman as we casually shared.

"Thanks," I answered.

"This is how it's supposed to be," she said dogmatically, her sweet smile suddenly hidden by a look of disapproval. "It just breaks my heart that girls today are having sex, and then think they can wear white!"

I began to feel foolish, thinking back to my own wedding and all the private conversations I'd had with myself about whether or not I deserved to wear white. In the end, I did wear it, but not confidently.

"You wait, then you wear white," she said, seemingly to lecture me.

She went on for a long, long time. With each word I felt more and more out of place . . . unworthy . . . hypocritical.

"Don't you agree?" she suddenly asked, coming up for breath. "Someone who's impure shouldn't wear white. They should be like you to wear white."

My heart fell into the pit of my stomach.

"Maybe you should read about me before you decide what you think," I said, offering her a simple magazine article that contained my story.

"I'd love to," she said, snatching it from me. "Maybe I'll find something in here to teach my daughter a thing or two."

With that, she was off, taking my confidence with her. Maybe she was right. Maybe I was setting myself up to look like a fool.

In a sea of people whose hearts and goals were the same, I suddenly felt like there was no one to talk to about who I really was. I spent the rest of the day wrestling with what that woman had said. It was the first of many similar conversations that threatened my very calling.

Have you ever noticed how comfortable church people in the West are talking about illness, accidents, and even death? We're happy to fix meals or even offer our heard-it-through-the-grapevine cure. But bring up sin and we're all a little nervous. Are we chefs? Doctors? No. We are Christians, and we're supposed to be in the business of helping people with their sin. If only this were commonly seen, perhaps fewer hearts would hide.

Let's begin with us. You and me. Maybe if we start to be about Christ overcoming sin, it will spread!

I'm going to ask you to shed that mask. I hope you are silly with anticipation to see what adventures God begins to bring your way, but I'm almost certain you're more aware of how difficult this task might be. Let's see if I can give you some courage. I'm not sure this is going to be a tender dose of courage, but I can promise it'll yield great things in your life. Can you stick with me?

Public Confession Is Foundational to Our Faith

Let's start with this truth: One of the distinctions of the Christian faith is public confession. Romans 10:9–10 says, "If you confess with your mouth, 'Jesus is Lord,' and believe in your heart that God raised him from the dead, you will be saved. For it is with your heart that you believe and are justified, and it is with your mouth that you confess and are saved." This is where we begin. With bold, verbal, who-cares-who-hears-it confession! New believers often become so eager for the release of confession that it gushes out. Our mouths must confess!

Now, I do understand that there is some discretion that must be used with public confession, whether it's coming to Christ for the first time or just realigning yourself to holiness. For example, it would not be wise for a mother who is just surrendering to Christ to dump her drug addiction, past abortion, and struggles with masturbation onto her twelve- and fifteen-year-olds. Sometimes the public confession will be cautious, but I firmly believe that there will be an appropriate relationship where specific confession can and should occur. The evidence that this has been properly accomplished will be the freedom you feel from obsession over particular sins. They won't be a deeply painful place or a repetitive pattern in your life anymore. Confession brings both healing and accountability.

Baptism Is Public Humility Concerning Our Need

Baptism further amplifies this public acknowledgment of sin. Did you know that in Bible days, water baptism was known among the Jews as a ritual for the truly unclean? Gentiles were baptized. Jews rarely were. It was considered a humiliating ritual. But even Jesus submitted to it as an example for us of how vital it is to make this public alignment of faith in God.

Mark 16:15–16 records Jesus' instructions to "go into all the world and preach the good news to all creation. Whoever believes and is baptized will be saved." The early believers took this seriously. They considered baptism to be the outward evidence of the inward sign that a person's heart had been circumcised to love God.

In fact, two of Christ's disciples, Paul and Silas, were in jail for their faith when an earthquake struck. In the rubble, the jailer was certain his prisoners had escaped and was about to kill himself, when the disciples cried out, "Don't harm yourself! We are all here." The jailer was so touched by this that he believed in Christ and confessed his sins right then and there. And it seems to have been *that very night* that the disciples baptized him. I wonder if we would be so committed to baptizing a new believer in the midst of such chaos? Probably not! I fear that all too many of us take baptism far too casually.

Public Confession Culminated in
Power Among the Believers

Acts 19:18–20 says, "Many of those who believed now came and openly confessed their evil deeds. A number who had practiced sorcery brought their scrolls together and burned them publicly. When they calculated the value of the scrolls, the total came to fifty-thousand drachmas [full day's wages]. In this way the word of the Lord spread widely and grew in power."

It seems that the early believers didn't waste time hiding sin as we do. And, their openness about their sins caused great growth for the kingdom. Now please understand that this doesn't appear to be a form of discipline. I've seen hearts made hard by forcing a public confession as a form of penance. I can't support that. Rather, this is those who desired to confess openly so that others would be wiser. And that's exactly what occurred. It also created accountability. If any of those ex-sorcerers ever had a day of weakness when they wanted to return to their scrolls, they need only turn for accountability to one of their friends who'd been at that great fire.

SHOULD I TELL MY HUSBAND?

I know this question is running through a lot of your minds right now. Should you tell your husband about past sexual sin? I wrote about that at length in my book *Pursuing the Pearl: The Quest for a Pure, Passionate Marriage.* I believe you should at some point confess any sexual sin to your husband. After all, it was a sin against him. But primarily my concern is that as you move into deeper spiritual intimacy—into the secret of the Lord—you'll want him to come along with you. It should always be our desire to move toward greater spiritual intimacy with our husbands. How can we be spiritually intimate with someone who doesn't know our deepest places of spiritual need and renewal?

Two exceptions would be a husband who struggles greatly with unforgiveness or one who is not a believer. In both of these cases, I would start with a wise mentor who has skill and knowledge about how to help facilitate confession at the right time, if ever.

My husband was the one to whom I first confessed ten years ago. He was the loving and forgiving secret of the Lord to me. My confession also brought him to a place of being ready to really work through issues of impurity that he was struggling with. The overall effect for us has been deeper spiritual intimacy and a greater friendship.

Where Do We Find Cautious Confession?

So, tell me. Where in Scripture do we find the luxury of being cautious with confession? I know the conventional wisdom of today's Western church is that allowing others to see sin in your life might cause them to take sin lightly. We're especially programmed to think that leaders shouldn't allow their sins to be known. Why, then, does 1 Timothy 5:20–21 say, "Those [church leaders] who sin are to be rebuked publicly, so that the others may take warning. I charge you, in the sight of God and Christ Jesus and the elect angels, to keep these instructions without partiality"?

Again, I'm not suggesting public discipline. (Although when leaders have an unrepentant heart, this passage does allow for that.) What I'm pleading for is that we have the humility of Paul, who called himself "the chief sinner." In Acts 20:19 he declares to the elders of the church of Ephesus that he "served the Lord with great humility and with tears." I thought it a tad funny that a humble man would mention his humility. Guess what? That's one of those places where our translations lose meaning. According to Beth Moore, the Greek word for *humility* was *tapeinophrosune*, which means "to confess sin with a deep realization of unworthiness."[1]

Paul didn't hide his sin. He was real with others about where he'd come from, and in this, his final address to the church of Ephesus, he was encouraging them to follow in his footsteps! He did not hide or ignore his sin, conveying an expectation to others that he was all but perfect. He celebrated God's rescue of him. We need to get real with each other about how very grateful we are for what Christ has rescued us from. And latch on to the healing and intimacy that's promised in that environment.

I have to ask you again, Where in Scripture do we find the luxury of being cautious with confession? We don't. The caution doesn't come from scriptural commands or even biblical preferences. So, what causes us to be so cautious?

Often it's pride.

Pride is the root of this next lie that I hear again and again and again. When I tell a young woman that she needs to confess her sin to someone in her congregation, the lie usually comes out something like this: "Well, there's really *no one* I can talk to."

"I could never tell my mom . . . pastor's wife . . . husband."

"I think I just need to confess it to God and that is enough."

The pride seems to be greatest among Christian leaders. They don't often verbalize the pride, but I can see it in their eyes. It would sound something like this. "But I'm the pastor's wife . . . the youth leader . . . a Sunday school teacher . . ." Now, that's a woman who struggles with pride.

Tammy Maltby, my friend and the contagiously fun host of television's *Aspiring Women*, writes in her book *Lifegiving* about a woman with sin in her life. We don't know her name, but we know her mask had been ripped to shreds. We meet her in Luke 7 where she's wetting Jesus' feet with her tears of repentance and pouring out her dreams to Him. Tammy writes:

> The Pharisee, Simon, implied that Jesus did not recognize the depth of this woman's depravity. Simon said to himself, "If this man were a prophet, he would know who is touching him and *what kind* of woman she is—that she is a sinner" (Luke 7:39 emphasis mine). The English words what kind in this verse are derived from two Greek words, poios, meaning "what," and dapedon, meaning "soil." In other words, Simon suggests that Jesus did not clearly comprehend that the "soil" of her life was made up of nothing but compost, dung, sinful muck, and shame-ridden manure. Her "soil" was clearly appalling to the Pharisee, but to the Savior, who takes the dead places of our lives and creates breathtaking beauty, her soil was just right.[2]

Tammy's teaching was an epiphany for me. I realized that Jesus doesn't see my past filth as something to hide; instead, He sees a most fertile place to plant. And, oh, if we let Him plant in such places, what fruit will grow! Why? Because the world will be able to see His power when we demonstrate how very powerless we've once been and how powerless we still are without Him.

This has become one of my favorite New Testament Bible stories. You see, I realize that I've been both the sinner woman *and* the Pharisee. In fact, like most women who can multitask . . . I've been them both at once! How's that for efficiency? These two—the sinner woman and the Pharisee—often intersect at this lie: "There's no one I can talk to."

> *"Fig leaves wouldn't hide Adam and Eve from God, and our modern forms of fig leaves won't protect us from the enemy. Surely it's more than coincidence that Satan is having his greatest field day over the very dimension of our lives that we are most reluctant to bring before God for help, healing and wholeness."*[3]
> —BETH MOORE

In the last few chapters, we've looked pretty closely at our tendency to be the sinner woman. We've all got some compost or junk in our lives. That's how we got to the point of needing to talk to someone. This brings us to our role as the Pharisee.

Oh, did the Pharisees wear masks! But they'd never admit it. They just claimed to be so righteous (think: *self*-righteous) that they wouldn't eat with sinners, wouldn't walk near places where they might run into sinners, and definitely wouldn't touch sinners. Above all, they never confessed to *being* sinners . . . at least, not publicly.

Jesus spent time with these self-righteous religious leaders, as you can see in this story. We have record that He confronted many of them with their sin. Not *once* do we see a Pharisee repenting in humility when confronted by Jesus. The key spiritual garb of those rule-abiding religious leaders was the mask, which they wore out of pride.

Are you getting my point here?

If you really think yourself above confessing your sin, then you're knowingly embracing the garb of the Pharisees. I hardly think that God's Word would encourage us to confess our sins one to another so that we "may be healed" (James 5:16) and then not give us someone to confess to. It's our pride that makes us think "there's no one to talk to."

If you see the Pharisee in yourself as I have in myself, take heart! Though none of Christ's confrontations resulted in a Pharisee taking off his mask, the Holy Spirit did break through one Pharisee's facade. Think! Can you recall a Pharisee who wrote many of the Bible's New Testament letters? Hint: He was probably the greatest missionary during the time of the New Testament Church. Hint-hint: I wrote about him sharing his sin just a few paragraphs ago. Got it? Yes, Paul was trained as a Pharisee! (Acts 23:6) This brings us really good news. Apparently when God gets hold of a Pharisee, He does big stuff!

Do not believe the lie that there is no one you can tell. God will provide that person. I believe this simply because His Word tells us that humble confession is one of the vital signs of a healthy believer.

This brings us to our final lie. Ever faced this one: "God has no use for me now"? It seems that with each lie we bust through, Satan has another one waiting. When we finally get our sin out on the table, this is the one that holds us back from the adventures of God. Well, I've got some truth that'll whack that one out of the ballpark! Join me for an exciting lesson in life-mapping!

✑— It's Your Turn —✎

Journaling can help you prepare to officially remove that mask of perfection to step into the secret of the Lord. How do you go about this kind of confession? Let me break it down into a few steps for you to make the process simpler and less painful if you are still feeling frightened. Just keep your journal nearby to write thoughts and names and ideas as I share these steps with you.

Step One: Pray
(Ask the Lord to Help You Identify This Person)

Pray about it. Our minds often rush to friends or obvious relationships. While the whole idea behind the secret of the Lord is having a *group* of people who walk in spiritual intimacy with you, it's often wise to first connect to someone who can mentor you for a while before you begin to open up to peers. He may have chosen someone for you who is not in your immediate circle of influence or who isn't an obvious match. One of my most valued peer confidantes is Suzy. She's a drum-playin', basketball shootin', dress-boycotting, absolute middle-aged tomboy. I'm pretty much a girl's girl who loves chick flicks, lip gloss, and bubble baths. When I first met Suzy, I'd have never imagined she would be one of my number one confidantes, but God knew! Just sit quietly and ask the Lord to give you some names to consider.

STEP TWO: SELECT
(CHOOSE SOMEONE YOU KNOW AND SEE OFTEN)

I deeply desire for you to find at least one ongoing relationship where you can grow in spiritual intimacy. That's not going to happen if you confess to a traveling speaker. Sometimes confessing to someone you'll never see again is a great jumping-off point and builds a lot of confidence, but it's not helping you enter into the secret of the Lord. If you select someone who does not run in your circle, be ready to reconfigure your life to create frequent contact.

If this is the first person you're confiding in, I'd really recommend you start with a mentor and not a peer. Select someone who's an older, wiser advisor who will have some perspective that you don't yet have. Unless you are confessing to your husband, the person you choose should be a woman.

STEP THREE: RENOUNCE
(SPEAK OUT AGAINST THIS SIN IN FRONT OF YOUR FRIEND)

Once you have figured out who to talk to, ask her to set aside some private time to help you talk through some issues and simply let it spill out. After you have spent some time sharing and hearing her advice, be sure to apply the truth of 2 Corinthians 4:2, which says, "We have *renounced* secret and shameful ways; we do not use deception, nor do we distort the word of God. On the contrary, by setting forth the truth plainly we commend ourselves to every man's conscience in the sight of God (emphasis mine)."

The Greek word for the word *renounce* is *apeipon,* which means "to speak out against." Here we go again! It seems that the mouth is pretty vital to overcoming sin. Ya know what I think? I think it loosens things up in the spiritual realm when we speak out against our sin. So, sit down with this new confidante—your first taste of the secret of the Lord—and speak out! Pray out loud in power and authority. Confess. Claim healing. Renounce!

You can't even imagine how good it's gonna feel! Oh, I'm praying for you, my friend. Be courageous! This really is the most painful part of entering into the secret of the Lord, but don't miss it. Adventure awaits!

CHAPTER SIX

Lie #3: "God Has No Use for Me Now"

*For I know the plans I have for you," declares the LORD,
"plans to prosper you and not to harm you,
plans to give you hope and a future.*

—JEREMIAH 29:11

I'm sorry," she confessed. It was the woman who'd emphasized how important it was to wear white only if you "deserved it." "I read your story, and I'm sorry. I must have really hurt you yesterday," she continued.

"It's OK," I answered, a little shocked.

"No, I am really sorry," she said as tears began to well in her eyes. "Seeing into your heart and feeling your hurt and shame really confronted my pride. I'm so ashamed."

I didn't know what to say. I was stunned. Was this the same woman?

Our conversation quickly turned into a private confession of her own fears and hurts. Before I knew it, I was comforting her. I was praying for her right out in the public eye.

It would be repeated time and time again. The judgment. The

fear. My true confession. God's unbelievable grace to turn things around and to use me, sin and all.

By the time I was twenty-eight, I had a few local and statewide purity retreats under my belt. At the first few, I didn't speak directly to the girls about my sin. I deeply regret that. I still believed the lie that if my sin was known, I couldn't be effective in serving God. Even after I'd seen the power of transparency, I often felt completely unworthy. It was never quite as pronounced as the day that older, gray-haired woman first spoke to me. I wrestled all night long, thinking I wasn't really obeying God. I was just setting myself up to make Him look bad. After all, I couldn't be really useful in His kingdom after falling like that, could I?

Have you ever believed that lie? Even in a small way? Maybe, like me, a sin kept you believing that lie. In your heart, you simply don't feel useful to God. Been there? Done that? Then get a load of this mind-boggling truth. Jeremiah 29:11 says, "'For I know the plans I have for you,' declares the LORD, 'plans to prosper you and not to harm you, plans to give you hope and a *future*'"(emphasis mine). Here's what Beth Moore has to say about the word *future* in that verse:

The Hebrew word for future includes the following explanation; its general meaning is "after, later, behind, following." The Hebrew way of thinking has been compared to a man rowing a boat; he backs into the future while looking toward where he has been. Therefore, what is "behind" and what is "future" come from the same root, "ahar."

Try to grasp this; God cherishes your heritage . . . Listen

carefully . . . You can't become the servant God is calling you to be without the threads of your past being knit into the Technicolor fabric of your future.[1]

Stop running from the past. You can't find the secret of the Lord until you lay your past on the altar with all your dreams for the future. Remember, you're giving God your future. Trusting Him to plan your dreams! And when you do, God will mix it with your gifts and passions as only He can.

There is a beautiful psalm that invites us into a deep, intimate, inner place of worship. It was written by the sons of Korah. To appreciate it, you have to know their past! Let's map out their lives and see their highs and lows.

HIGH #1: A SPECIAL APPOINTMENT

In Numbers 4 the sons of Korah get an appointment from God. They're called to carry the tabernacle and its holy articles through the wilderness. When the Lord was ready to move them, Aaron and the other priests would gather up the articles and first wrap them. Then the Kohathites would carry them without directly touching them. You see, if they touched them directly or walked into the holy dwelling, they would die. Still, very few were even allowed the honor of carrying the wrapped articles of the tabernacle. This appointment was probably a "high" point for them as it carried far more honor than most of the Israelites had.

Low: Jealousy Sets In

But soon we see a "low" recorded in Numbers 16. Jealousy sets in. You see, the Kohathites are literally cousins of Aaron—descendants of the Levitical priesthood. Jealousy begins to creep in as they ponder dangerous questions. Why couldn't they go into the courts of God? Why couldn't they touch the holy articles? It didn't make sense. They wanted a different appointment.

Korah, one of the Kohathites, gathers about 250 men to rise up and confront Moses, saying, "You have gone too far! The whole community is holy, every one of them, and the LORD is with them. Why then do you set yourselves above the LORD's assembly?" (v. 3). Moses pleads with him to be content with the position God has assigned to his family, but Korah will not settle. He wants a greater gift. He wants total access to the Holy of Holies.

Moses leaves the judging up to God. (Wise idea when you're being confronted like this.) He says that if the men die naturally, then the Lord did not appoint him (Moses) to lead. However, if the ground swallows them up, all of Israel will know that the men were testing God's will. Just then, an earthquake swallows them, their houses, and all their belongings! Just them—no one else! (I guess that'd be a low, huh?)

High #2: The Remnant of Korah's Family Obeys . . . and Sings About It

Not all of Korah's family rise up against Moses, and so some continue on with the work assigned. All the while, they do crave the full glory of God's inner court. But they've learned from their father's sin, and they embrace their role. In Psalm 84:10 they write, "I would rather be a doorkeeper in the house of my God than dwell in the tents of the wicked." They're just doorkeepers and that's OK with them even though they still crave God's glory. They just don't want to revel in the tents of wickedness as their father had. And right then . . . the thread of their past is woven into a special gift they have. Music. If you know it, sing with me the contemporary worship song based on Psalm 84, written by the sons of Korah.

> How lovely is your dwelling place,
> Oh Lord Almighty
> For my soul longs and even faints for you
> And here my heart is satisfied . . .
> Better is one day in your courts
> Better is one day in your house
> Better is one day in your courts
> Than thousands elsewhere.

This is another high for them. They're being used through many writings recorded in the Psalms to teach others the craving of God's glory!

Does God continue to use them? Yep! They retain their position as mere doorkeepers and write songs about craving God's glory. It is the very emotional place of their family's past sin that God uses to write these songs.

Remember, Aaron had actually been in the Holy of Holies. He had seen God's glory. Couldn't God have used Aaron to write about God's glory? He could have. But he didn't. He used those whose forefathers had sinned in their quest for it. He used those whose hearts were broken by the sin of unrighteouslessly claiming God's presence. They glorified God not by hiding their family sin, but by embracing the pain of it and dragging it into the light for everyone to see God's redemption and forgiveness. Who better to call us into the craving of God's presence than those who had sinned in their quest to taste of it?

Second Corinthians 1: 3–4 says, "Praise be to the God and Father of our Lord Jesus Christ, the Father of compassion and the God of all comfort, who comforts us in all our troubles, so that we can comfort those in any trouble with the comfort we ourselves have received from God." God doesn't heal us from our sin just to sit us on the sidelines. He healed the sons of Korah so they could pour their craving for God into others. Have you a story of brokenness? Just imagine how much healing God could pour out through your life.

Our Victory: God Uses Our Past

I once believed that God could not use me because of my sexual sin. Instead, I've found that He uses me because of it. Who better to plead with today's teens than one who knows the devastation of sexual sin? Who better to help the approximately 42 percent of women in the body of Christ who have sexual pain in their past, than one who has successfully navigated the path of healing?

It amazes me that when I am with teenage girls, I'm often able to pick out the one who's wounded by sexual pain. She can be giggling with the rest, but there's just a knowing I have. I can't fully explain it, and I don't barge up to her and confront her. I wait for God's Spirit to do the connecting. My heart bleeds with these young women to find hope. And I know just how to lead them there. It's familiar territory. Just as the sons of Korah knew how to raise up a craving in someone's heart to go into a deeper place with God, I know how to raise up the healing of sexual pain and the passionate quest for purity. It is built into the fabric of my life. It is my story.

What's yours? What wonderful rescue story has God written with your life?

I'm not telling you that you'll need to broadcast your sin. I'm telling you that you need to be willing to let God's Spirit help you discern who needs to hear your story or borrow your strength. Maybe you'll not use your specific testimony, but the mercy that God developed through your pain. Maybe the journey God took you on to overcome cigarettes is the same formula He'll use in a friend's life to help her overcome soap operas! Maybe the same path you took to forgive your mom for verbal abuse will be the one your friend needs to walk to forgive her uncle for sexual abuse. Whose life is God going to redeem through your humility? I can't wait to see.

It's all about our stories . . . including the ones that make us feel utterly worthless. These stories, when relinquished to God's power, are our proof that God is. I cannot see the wind, but I know that it is because I can see it touching trees and causing them to dance. So it is with God. I cannot see Him, but I know He is because I've seen Him touching lives and causing them to dance. I can only see this through the stories I hear. And, oh, how I do love to hear them.

What's yours?

> *"We are all pencils in the hand of a writing God,*
> *who is sending love letters to the world."*[2]
> —MOTHER TERESA

✌ IT'S YOUR TURN ✌

This exercise will take some time, but I've found that it is worth it. In fact, I consider it to be one of the most powerful parts of this book. We're going to map out your life story. Some women have cried when they were able to see God's precious hand on their life stories as they mapped out their "highs" and "lows." What I want to help you see is that God threads everything together . . . including your sin.

I did this almost ten years ago at the prompting of the Spirit. I saw two threads. The first was that I adored teaching God's Word. Here are the places where I saw that thread:

High: I came to know Christ in a Child Evangelism Fellowship 5-Day Club

High: I was a summer missionary for Child Evangelism Fellowship

Low: I found elementary education as my major in college a great disappointment

Mid-high: Though the material didn't impassion me, I loved being a corporate trainer in the first few years of my career

The second thread I saw was this:

Low: A conversation with my mother about sexual sin when I was a tweenager moved me deeply

Deep Low: My sexual sin

Low: The mask I wore for ten years as a result of my sexual sin

High: Confessing my sin to my husband, Bob

Here's kind of what my life map would look like:

We are all pencils in the hand of a writing God who is sending love letters to the world.

Came to know Christ

Summer Missionary

Confessing my sin

Elementary Education

Corporate Trainer

The Conversation

My Sexual Sin

The 10-year Mask

See the threads being pulled together? Of course there were lots of other highs and lows on my life map, but they didn't connect into meaningful threads. God has used my passion for teaching and the personal wisdom gained about sexuality to create a fabulous purpose for me, and my past sin is deeply woven into it. He uses it.

What are your treasured "highs"? What are your difficult, sinful "lows"? I want you to draw a life map in your journal for your own life similar to the one I drew for myself. Yours should be far more detailed and longer so you can catch every significant event. Watch to see how God may be running a common thread through them.

I want you to sit down and concentrate on this prayerfully for a good length of time today, but you'll find that it is something you come back to for many days or, perhaps, even longer. When developing my life map, God lovingly brought things to mind as I pondered this project for many weeks.

Here are some prayers to lift as you begin to plot your highs and lows during this first intensive session:

"Lord Jesus Christ, I yield my mind to You and You alone for this significant exercise. Please remove all clutter and distractions from me, and do not let the enemy create fear or misdirect me. I desire to see how You would use my past to glorify You and ask that You allow anything that You don't want used to fall to the ground and die."

"Lord Jesus Christ, please reveal to me any significant spiritual events that need to be on this timeline. Don't let me miss one single spiritual high, such as when I came to know

You, when I've surrendered my life in significant ways, or when I received words from You about my life. Let me be unafraid to transparently map any significant spiritual lows, including my moments of deepest shame and sin. Let me see moments of my own sin that I need to weave into my purpose or moments of sin committed against me that You intend to use for Your glory."

"Lord Jesus Christ, please reveal to me any significant emotional highs and lows *such as achievements, passions and pleasures, hurts and disappointments. Do not let me miss one single emotional high or low, but give me courage to recall them and record them. Let me see how You have been weaving these emotional times into my life purpose for Your glory!"*

PART THREE

The Fear of God

CHAPTER SEVEN

The Fear of Man

God resists the proud.
—1 Peter 5:5 (nkjv)

Since I was fourteen, I desired to write. And after several years of writing ad copy, corporate brochures, and marketing plans, God awakened a new passion in me. I wanted to write my story for teen girls. I wanted them to see that they were not alone when they messed up or when they stood for purity. I could see that no matter what side of the road they were on, they felt alone.

After I had fasted and prayed, God seemed to have confirmed that this passion was from Him. I even had my husband's nod of approval. There was just one thing holding me back.

What on earth would my daddy think?

I'd never told him. I wasn't sure if I was willing to, and if that meant forfeiting this desire to write, I was willing to do that.

"The secret of the LORD is with them that fear him; and he will shew them his covenant." I love this verse. (As if you haven't noticed!) I think this is the right time to remind you how powerful it is. We're headed to a place of tremendous reviving power, with Psalm 25:14 paving the way. Malcolm Smith, author of *The Lost Secret of the New Covenant*, says, "This may be one of the most amazing verses in the Bible, putting into one sentence the incredible plan God has purposed for mankind."[1] Do you want God's plan for your life to unfold? Then let's move on with our quest for the secret of the Lord.

We've already discovered that this is a tight-knit body of believers who aren't afraid to confront *and* comfort when sin is in the picture. These are people who celebrate the good stuff and grieve the sad stuff. They are a mask-free body of believers who know one another so intimately that they are like a secret.

But how do you get into the secret of the Lord? It's obvious that taking our masks off is part of it, but what gives us the strength to do such a task? The fear of God.

Our Western world doesn't have a foundation to easily understand the fear of God. So I want to take a kind of backward approach to this concept of fearing God.

THE FEAR OF MAN: THE OPPOSITE OF FEARING GOD

When I first became hungry for the intimacy of the secret of the Lord, I read that second phrase and I pleaded, "Fear You? How can I fear You? Lord, I'm crazy about You. Everything good in my life is from You. What do You mean by fear You?"

I cracked open my Hebrew dictionary to find that the word in that verse for fear is *yara*. It means "to stand in awe of, to submit to, to bow before, to worship."

I remember well the prayer that I prayed when I first read the Hebrew definition for *fear/yara*. "Well, of course I want to worship You, God! Show me what this means. I don't get it."

I closed my eyes.

At that moment I saw myself bowing down and worshipping, but it wasn't God before me! In my head I saw myself standing in awe of, submitting to, bowing before, and worshipping man. How grieving this picture was, but as only God can teach us, I knew this was a true picture of how I often lived.

Have you ever decided not to visit the family whose kid just got taken in for drug sales because you were *afraid* they might be offended or embarrassed . . . and all the while God tugged at your heart to reach out? Have you ever not spoken up to a couple who was separating to tell them that as believers that's just not a good decision . . . maybe you were *afraid* you wouldn't know exactly what to say or afraid they'd feel judged . . . but it was clear that God put it on your conscience to speak truth? Have you ever failed to speak up at the hair salon when the workers talked about living with their boyfriends because you were *afraid* you might not be effective or look intelligent . . . but the Holy Spirit kept pushing you to say something?

Have you ever not confessed sin that seemed to keep rotting a hole of pain and isolation into your heart because you were *afraid* of what people would think if they really knew . . . even though God has made it clear to you that confession is the path to healing, accountability, and the power to overcome? Instead of moving forward in submissive obedience to His call, we often sit around and worry about what others think!

From the time I was fifteen until the day I confessed my sin to my husband when I was twenty-five, I was deeply convicted that I needed to tell someone about my sin. Why didn't I? I was afraid of what others might think. I was covered in the fear of man. I was afraid that if my mask came off, others wouldn't find me acceptable. I was afraid I might be a sidelined, "lesser" believer if they knew. I was afraid my husband would reject me. All the while, God kept prodding me to tell someone about my shame.

See how "fearing God" is a precious piece of the secret of the Lord? Only when we fear God will we have the courage to shed our masks. Once we do that, God begins to re-dream with us, calling us to new and exciting ministry appointments. That's when the fear of man intrudes again.

Fear of my dad almost kept me from stepping out to write *And the Bride Wore White,* my first book. My daddy loves me, protects me, advises me, watches out for me, and is crazy about me. My fear was completely irrational, but equally gripping. I was very close to relinquishing God's call on my life out of fear of what my dad would think if he knew my shame. One day, I finally told my mom of my fear and she promised to walk me through it. She did. The day *And the Bride Wore White* was released, my dad was not ashamed or broken or disappointed. He was proud to the very core. I felt it.

At the very heart of it, we are choosing who we bow to . . . man or Jesus. Peer pressure, which you and I haven't entirely outgrown, is really submitting to . . . standing in awe of . . . bowing before . . . *worshipping* man.

THE FEAR OF MAN IS COMPLETELY IRRATIONAL

Recently, I was at a hotel simply to get this book finished. I spent almost four days in this place and experienced what I can only call excruciating writer's block. I had never had this before. I feared perhaps I was never going to write another sentence, let alone another book. It didn't make sense. All the research was there, but I couldn't get one sentence down on paper.

I prayed. I fasted. And I stared at an empty screen for hours on end.

I was frustrated and took frequent poolside breaks from the lack of progress. During one such break, I met a dear towel attendant—a middle-aged man with dark curly hair, a heavy New York accent, and leathery tanned skin. It seemed to me he'd spent a lot of years working at this place. He wasn't like you or me. He kind of had his own language. His own world. He reminded me of Dustin Hoffman's character in the 1980s movie *Rainman*. Hoffman played an autistic middle-aged guy who drove his brother nuts with random knowledge and facts and figures, but made little to no emotional connection.

Like Rainman, he seemed brilliant. Someone would walk up with a Patriots T-shirt on, and he'd begin calling Patriots plays like a practiced commentator. He'd see two young lovebirds walking hand in hand, and his lips would begin to sing, "Let me call you Sweetheart." He just smiled when people told them their needs, and then he'd do whatever they'd ask, all the while talking about the Steelers or the city or Rome or whatever may have been on someone's T-shirt. He spoke *about* us, but not really *to* us. He seemed content, happy, and even . . . well, simple in his little world.

On one particular morning, I was sitting on my hotel balcony enjoying some conversation with my Savior when I felt the Lord say, "Pray for the towel guy." I did. Then, I felt Him say, "Now, go tell him you've just prayed for him and ask him if he knows Me." I was immediately struck with complete fear. What would he think of me? What would others at the pool think of me?

That is the fear of man. It's not even rational. Why on earth would an intelligent, middle-aged, well-conversed woman fear a man such as this towel guy . . . so sweet and innocent and simple? But I was racked with fear. I wrestled with God until finally I just got my stuff and marched myself down to the pool. "God, help me," I whispered as I approached the sweet towel guy.

"Hi," I said.

He didn't answer. He began to walk past me and mumbled the first statement I'd ever heard him say that related to the here and now.

"Oh, I wish this day was ova," he croaked in his thick accent.

"Are you having a bad day?" I asked.

He looked at me for the first time all week.

"Yeah," he sighed, quickly looking down at his feet. He was talking to me! Really communicating. Perhaps even connecting!

"That's funny," I said. "I was just in my room, and God told me to pray for you, and I did. I think your day will get better now."

He smiled! He looked at me. He connected!

"Do you know Jesus?" I asked.

"Hallelujah," he said, going back into his little world of imitation. "Praise the Lord. Yep. Yep. Praise the Lord." He mimicked words he'd obviously heard on television and began to deeply recede into his world again.

That was it. No dramatic prayer session. No big ending. I walked back to my room a little disappointed, not knowing if this sweet man knew Jesus or not.

Do you know what happened next? I went back to my room and suddenly started pounding out words with passion. My heart was simply fluttering. I had to stop to sing to the Lord from time to time. Just like when I was fifteen . . .

I had butterflies!

I told my husband, Bob, this story, and he kept waiting for the "punch line." That "aha" moment when something supernatural occurred. But there wasn't one. Simple obedience that day didn't produce a miracle right then and there. But I planted a seed in obedience that I hope others will water in obedience. As a result God released much of this book. It all came down to simple obedience.

Sadly, we are a society that doesn't like obedience or respect for authority or anything that makes us look powerless. Rather, we are plagued with the overwhelming desire to be pleasing and self-sufficient in the eyes of man. We worry endlessly about what others will think about decisions we make, the house we live in, the car we drive, the church we attend, and how our kids act.

At its core, this is simply idolatry. We are submitting to, standing in awe of, bowing down to, and worshipping man.

THE FEAR OF MAN CAUSES GOD TO RESIST US

I promised you earlier that entering the secret of the Lord would awaken the enemy. Ever feel like the enemy is thwarting every attempt in your life to accomplish something? Maybe you're a student who keeps getting into bad relationship after bad relationship and you feel like a victim after each trashing, even though you've chosen to join with guys who couldn't care less about God. Maybe you're a mom who feels that your teenage daughter is just never going to turn out right despite your high standards, but you've failed to obey God in slowing down and focusing on her instead of your career. Maybe you're feeling called to a new and exciting, God-sized task, but the doors just keep slamming in your face, and you blame it on the devil even though you cannot remember the last time that you humbly confessed any sin. Though it is possible that it is spiritual warfare that you face, don't be too quick to blame the enemy.

IS GOD RESISTING YOUR REQUEST
FOR A HEALED MARRIAGE?

I realize that not all women who read this book are married. Well, I hope some aren't, because I deeply desire to minister to single and college-aged women through its message so that you don't waste years on the sidelines! If you are single, take heart. I'm praying for you, too, but I need to direct a little message to those who are married.

While we're reviving you, it's likely that we'll revive your marriage. Until ten years ago, not only did I need revival . . . my marriage needed revival. Oh, I'd prayed for years and years, but nothing changed. Then one day, I picked up a copy of Stormie Omartian's *The Power of a Praying Wife*. The most profound truth that came to me from that book is that before I could pray for God to revive my marriage, I had to ask Him to revive me. In other words, I had to see my own sin and humbly confess it before my prayers for God to cleanse Bob of his could be answered.

Have you been praying and praying and praying for God to fix your husband only to find He doesn't answer you? God truly does resist the proud. As much as He loves the marriage covenant, He will rarely work on your husband until you're willing to let Him fix you! Grab a copy of Stormie's book and start praying, "Lord, change *me!*"

One of my favorite Bible teachers, Pastor Erlo Stegan from South Africa, recently introduced me to a crucial truth to consider from James 4:6 and 1 Peter 5:5 (NKJV). They echo, "God resists the proud, but gives grace to the humble." God *resists* the proud.

God RESISTS!

God RESISTS!

Just imagine Him as your opposition! Whom would you call on? What other power is there? None! And yet when God sees pride in our lives, He Himself resists us.

Sometimes breakthrough is not a matter of hair-raising warfare prayer, but a simple matter of something we don't like to talk about in the West anymore: obedience. Sometimes the power of God holds us back until we're ready, in humility, to simply obey even at the cost of what others might think.

How about you? Are you finding your life filled with the overwhelming power of God? Spilling over the brim with the freshness of God's Spirit? Or are you just wondering why nothing ever happens? Do you find yourself constantly asking people to pray for you because you are being "attacked" by the enemy? Let's just consider another option. Could it be that God is resisting your pride?

Do you fear Him?

Or do you find yourself sometimes fearing man?

In this chapter we looked a bit at the opposite of fearing God . . . fearing man. I did that because this is how God taught me to understand the fear of Him. Now, let's turn our minds to exactly what the fear of God looks like!

> *"The world can do nothing to a Christian who has no fear of man."*[2]
> —BROTHER YUN

It's Your Turn

Identify a time recently when you did not fear God, but feared man. I have one! And I'm really ashamed of it. I was sitting in a public place working on this book. (Yes, I was writing about fearing God!) A middle-aged woman sat down near me with a book on psychic power. Immediately, I felt God nudging me to talk to her. "Tell her that psychic stuff is just a counterfeit," He prodded. He even gave me the words to say to her. I felt uncomfortable. Wondered what she'd think of me. Shamefully, I soon left, having never spoken a word to that woman. That's bowing to man. Oh, how we need to confess those moments. Why? Because God deeply wants us to learn from those moments so we remember to fear Him next time. Can you think of a time recently that you need to confess?

CHAPTER EIGHT

The Fear of God

Fear the LORD, you his saints,
for those who fear him lack nothing.
—PSALM 34:9

California. Canada. Australia. Africa. The letters were coming from every corner of the globe.

For so many years, I pleaded with God to use me to mentor women within my own little church. I didn't know where the desire came from, just that it was there. I also knew I hadn't been used.

He didn't choose me.

I brought all the best of me to the table, but He didn't choose me. With my Christian college degree, my years of experience in leading Bible studies, and my picture-perfect life, I was overlooked.

Now I offered one thing. The ugly story of my former sin and the wonderful way God had rescued me emotionally and spiritually. And I was chosen.

Not chosen to mentor a woman in my Bible study.

Not chosen to disciple a group of girls from my church.

Not even chosen to influence many in my neighborhood.

God was inexplicably taking the story of a sinful woman—who had no platform, no ministry, no media to promote a book—to many parts of the world.

How ironic His choices are.

The fear of God is the opposite of the fear of man, which is when we bow down to man's approval. Forgive me for starting backward, but every time I speak to audiences about the fear of God, this seems to be where everyone gets it. We've all been there. We've all bowed down to the whims of man.

Now that we know what it's not, what is it? Well, our key verse teaches us that the secret of the Lord is with us, *if* we fear God. So the secret of the Lord is a blessing that results from having this "fear" in our lives. So first it is an avenue of blessing.

The Fear of God Yields Blessings

There are many other wonderful outcomes from fearing God.

> "Who, then, is the man that fears the Lord?
> He [God] will instruct him in the way chosen for him."
> —Psalm 25:12

(The Lord shows us His plan for our lives if we fear Him.)

"How great is your goodness, which you have stored up
for those who fear you."
—PSALM 31:19

*(The Lord allows His goodness to flow in our lives if we
fear Him.)*

"He fulfills the desires of those who fear him."
—PSALM 145:19

*(The Lord brings the desires of our hearts to pass if we fear
Him.)*

"A woman who fears the LORD is to be praised."
—PROVERBS 31:30

(He protects our reputations if we fear Him.)

"Fear the LORD, you his saints,
for those who fear him lack nothing."
—PSALM 34:9

(Every single need in our lives is met if we fear Him.)

I could go on. These are just a few examples. My point, it's definitely something worth pursuing. Remember that because fearing Him is not always easy. You may be called to start ministries that your family doesn't understand. You may be called to visit people whom others do not approve of. You may be called to embrace truth that makes others uncomfortable. Fearing God is rarely easy.

It is, however, your doorway to great spiritual blessing, authority, and provision.

WHAT DOES IT ACTUALLY MEAN TO FEAR HIM?

Remember, the word *yara* means "to stand in awe, to submit to, to bow before, to worship." Obviously this isn't just talking about the best Sunday morning singing you've ever experienced. It's talking about a scope of worship beyond musical notes and chords. It's talking about a life of worship.

I learned a little about worship on New Year's Eve at Times Square a few years back. If you've never been, don't go. You've pretty much got to be drunk to tolerate the below-zero temperatures that New York usually gets around midnight at the turn of the year. I wasn't, so I felt the cold to my inner core.

My brother, Darin, was living in the Big Apple at the time. Bob and I thought it'd be such a wonderful memory to spend New Year's Eve at "the" party of the year. Darin knew how to get us right to the core of the party. He'd scheduled us to attend a musical in a theater on Times Square that let out at eleven, so we'd be right in the middle of the action at just the right time. We left the theater and there we were. Just on the edge of Times Square. The cameras. The big ball. The crowd.

The crowd!

For as far as the eye could see there was a sea of people, separated every half block by an enormous wall of police officers.

"What's with the officers?" I shouted to Darin over the crowd.

"These people will crush themselves if the officers don't separate them every so often," he shouted back. "They all want to be in the middle of Times Square . . . hundreds of thousands of them."

I believed him.

The drunken guy next to me shouted at an officer a few feet ahead. "Hey, pig, let us through," he slurred.

"Yeah, move that *&!$ fence of yours," came another sloppy speaker.

A few others joined in, adding their own brand of expletives and teaching me a few I'd never heard before. This was not a happy crowd. They were mad!

We stood there for a long time, just waiting and freezing. Everyone had their heads down and their hands in their pockets, trying to keep warm.

Where are the happy people you always see on TV? I wondered.

Suddenly, a great spotlight flooded my eyes and the people went wild with excitement, as if they'd been partying all along. They threw on their party hats, shouted, blew on party horns, and cheered . . . for all of ten seconds as the camera panned the scene. Then they went right back to warming their hands and occasionally cussing at the officers. This was not just a mad crowd. These people were crazy!

"Maybe we should leave," I shouted above the crowd.

"Too late!" Darin shouted back, knowingly. "No way out until midnight."

I held tightly to Bob on one side and Darin on the other. And I prayed. Hard!

As midnight approached, our little band of barricaded drunks got nastier and nastier to the officers in front of us. Well trained, those men of the NYPD never lost their cool. They kept silent.

"We're comin' through at midnight, pig," threatened a guy right next to me.

"Ten . . ."

The crowd began to push forward. It began to sway back and forth in rhythm with the countdown.

"Nine . . ."

"Lock arms," shouted Darin. We did.

"Eight . . ."

Darin's eyes scanned the terrain. "Don't let go. No matter what, don't let go!" he shouted.

"Seven . . ."

I was moving, but my feet weren't on the ground any longer. I was suspended between Darin and Bob, who were fighting with everything they had to keep me off the ground, because it was littered with broken beer bottles.

"Six . . ."

Bodies began to try to crush through me.

"Five . . ."

"Steady, hold tight!" shouted Darin. "Stay with me! Be ready!"

"Four . . ."

The crowd suddenly jumped forward a few feet.

"Now!" he screamed. He dodged and pushed and pressed along with Bob until we were into an alley just a few feet wide. A handful of scraggly teens were crowded into the alley, a puff of smoke above their heads.

"Three . . ."

"Two . . ."

"One . . ."

And the drunken crowd kept its promise! The barricade fell. The cops began falling. It wasn't a pretty sight. I wondered how many people got hurt. I was thankful that I wasn't one of them.

I stood there in the alley, expecting to rest awhile, my heart beating wildly. I began sniffing . . . sniffing an odd smell.

"Don't sniff," Darin instructed. "We'll only be here a moment." Soon the whole crowd was past us.

"Now!" Darin shouted again and, to my surprise, pulled us off in a great hurry. We went through a maze of alleys and streets.

"What was that strange smell?" I asked later.

"Pot, Dannah!" he said. "That was pot! That's why we weren't stickin' around."

What an education that night was! And what a lesson in worship. You see, I had to completely submit myself to my brother. I never for a moment questioned that we'd be OK. (Well, maybe for a brief moment when my feet weren't touching the ground.) I just moved in obedience to every instruction he offered us. He knew the streets. I didn't.

That's kind of what worship is like. I submitted to my brother because I knew he was better able to navigate me through that terrifying night. Worship is submitting to the One who knows. But we don't do that so well. We don't submit to God. Instead, we worry. We worry a lot.

> *"We cannot call him Lord
> and then proceed to run our own lives."* [1]
> —NANCY LEIGH DEMOSS

JUST SUBMIT AND FOLLOW!

This is where our Western mind-set gets in the way. We are humanistic. We think that we should be free to rule and run our own lives and to determine our own rights and wrongs. Even Christians have minds that have been transformed into humanistic philosophies. We do not, as a daily act of consciousness, submit to the hierarchy of the kingdom of God.

We don't like the fact that we're called to be His servants. We don't want to actually obey God. We just want to borrow His power from time to time. But until we submit and relinquish our own power, we'll never really get much of His.

God knows the terrain. He knows what positions to assume. Submitting to His orders is worship at its truest core.

Author John Eldredge takes an interesting approach in his teachings about God's authority and ours. He refers to our initial order from God to "Be fruitful and increase in number; fill the earth and subdue it" (Gen. 1:28). The same passage goes on to command clearly that man is to rule over the earth and its animals.

> And let them *rule*. Like a foreman runs a ranch or like a skipper runs a ship. Better still, like a king rules a kingdom, God appoints us as the governors of his domain. We were created to be the kings and queens of the earth (small *k*, small *q*). Hebrew scholar Robert Alter has looked long and hard at this passage, mining it for its riches. He says the idea of *rule* means "a fierce exercise of mastery." It is active, engaged, passionate. It is *fierce*. I suppose such language doesn't fit if we were created to spend our days

singing in the choir ("I may never march in the infantry"). But it makes perfect sense if we were born into a world at war. God says, "It will not be easy going. This is no Sunday school hour. Rule fiercely in my name." We were meant to rule, as he—the God of angel armies—rules![2]

This is no worrywart state of mind. This is a state of mind that has a certainty that God "is" and that He is sovereign. This state of mind is completely warlike. There's not room for hesitancy in warfare. You just obey. And without question. Why? Because it would be potentially life-threatening not to obey—for you and for others.

Mother Teresa was a woman who feared God. I most love her rescue of a small group of mentally and physically impaired children from the war-torn streets of Beirut. In the midst of a terrible scene with bombs exploding in the background, she approached the political authorities and requested permission to enter the war zone so that she could rescue the children from one specific hospital. The authorities were kind. After all, she was old and not politically savvy. They assured her that they could not allow it, as all would be killed driving those streets. She humbly and matter-of-factly asked again, telling them that this was what God wanted her to do. They explained that only if there was a cease-fire could she enter the war zone, but they told her that was not going to happen anytime soon. She assured them that she would ask God to make it happen. She did not plead for them to make it happen. She simply told them she believed God would make it happen.

Can you imagine speaking such a thing in the face of violent war? Would your faith be big enough? Would your courage be strong enough to look the fool? I have to confess, as I watch the video footage of that meeting, it is easy in my flesh to see a small, frail old woman who just does not understand the ways of the world.

But she did understand the ways of the kingdom world. She was a queen (small *q*) of the kingdom, and she would ask the King. Knowing Him as she did, she knew He would delight in answering yes to this selfless and loving request, even in the face of the anger and will of man.

The cease-fire occurred within twenty-four hours. It was inexplicable. It made no sense. The next day Mother Teresa drove through the bomb-ravaged but eerily quiet streets of Beirut to rescue thirty-seven little ones. Little ones who could not walk or speak to thank her. In the video footage of Mother Teresa rescuing those children, I see a queen of the kingdom taking authority as she worships the King by obeying Him in the streets of Beirut.

Get this. God knows the streets. He knows the best way through the chaos of our lives. And, since He's extended the authority of His kingdom to us, the usual way the world sees His power is through us. Do your friends see a woman who's confident about God's control over your life even in difficult times? Do they see a woman moving in obedient and submissive power to the authority of her King? Or do they see a contemporary, worrywart, overstretched, humanistic Western woman?

Worship is not a song. Worship is an everyday act of submitting to God in every moment of life. We experience His power best in the moments of chaos, but not when we take control of our own lives. When we worship—submit to His plans—we experience the reality!

Are you a worshipper?

THE STREETS OF MY LIFE

There are a lot of "streets" in my life. Before I took off my mask, I preferred to walk on the lovely streets filled with boutiques and ice cream stands—the MainStreetUSA-looking kind of streets. These streets had billboards advertising my Christian upbringing, my good works, my intelligence and skill, and even my "sacrifice" to go to a Christian college and turn my radio stations (which I then owned) over to God by taking off offensive lyrics and stuffing in an occasional Christian recording artist.

God had a different idea. He wanted me to walk through the gutter alleys of my life first. Those were streets I didn't want to walk. I had to walk past the stench of my sin, through the fear of my inability to protect myself from what others would think, and past the cluttered reality of massive sin in the body of Christ.

When I was willing to walk on those streets, God opened doors to streets I didn't even know existed. (Oh, I can't wait to share with you the next dream God gave to me. He keeps asking us to re-dream. Once we've settled into one dream, He invites us to walk through the exciting streets of adventure to another!)

◯— It's Your Turn —◯

Accepting God's free gift of salvation is our first surrender to God. It is the ultimate act of worship to embrace Jesus Christ for the first time, but our worship does not end at that point. No, it is just beginning. It is our pleasure from that moment on to live our lives in gratitude to a God who sees our sin and loves us and accepts us in spite of it. The fear of God should be born out of gratitude for that. Submit to Him by bowing the knee to Him today, no matter what street He asks you to take. In your journal, record a specific step . . . just one specific step . . . that you can take to worship God by walking in obedience down a street you are certain He is calling you to walk.

CHAPTER NINE

The Reward of Fearing God

*If you, O LORD, kept a record of sins, O LORD,
who could stand? But with you there is forgiveness;
therefore you are feared.*

—PSALM 130:3–4

This feeling was familiar. I knew it was the beginning of something, though I did not know exactly what. I'd felt it before, but not in
a long while. When was it that I felt this? Of course! It was when God
prompted me to write a book for teenagers about my past. This was the
same feeling.

Anticipation mingled with uncertainty. Passion met a new
dream. Faith rose up expecting a test. I was being called.

In the days and weeks to come, it seemed that everywhere I looked
I saw Africa. My mind whirred. Perhaps if I could touch the hearts of
teens in America, I could touch the hearts of teens in the countries of
Africa where HIV/AIDS seeks to devour so many.

"There are others already there. Others like Bruce Wilkinson,
Oprah Winfrey, Rick Warren," said a reluctant voice in my head.

"They have money and connections . . . and names. What do you have? You have nothing. You are too small. You can barely keep up with this growing ministry in the U.S. What are you thinking? This is all you are called to. Stick to this. Stay here."

I almost laughed. I'd heard that voice before. I would not listen to it.

"Lord, I don't have any money to go to Africa. I don't know anyone in Africa. I'm not famous, and I don't have a lot of power. I have no clear reason to go, but I hear Your call," I prayed. *"If it is Your voice, take me."*

I began to make plans. I was certain that if we kept on course, we could pay for a trip to Africa ourselves the following summer. Maybe if we could get there, we'd find the doorway to fulfill the call. I was sure it was His will that I go right away. It was not.

Instead, it was His will that my husband and I be refined. The next two years would be the most painful of our married lives.

Sin. Repentance.

Gossip. Hard truth.

Tears. Intimate nights of holding each other.

Lost friendships. Isolation. Loneliness.

The months passed by slowly.

Fearing God. It never seems to come easily. But when it comes, it brings such sweet rewards.

What I thought was a call to Africa—a bigger task than I'd ever dreamed of—awakened the enemy. And God, in His tender love to see me grow up as a believer, allowed it.

Bob and I have shared very openly about this period in our lives and will continue to do so when God prompts us to. From the very beginning it was our desire to be open, transparent, and truthful. When that has been allowed, it has brought healing to so many. However, the Lord tells us in 1 Corinthians 13:7 that love "protects." The Greek language actually says, "love covers in silence." This means that when we know about someone else's sin, we cover it in silence. We protect her. (That brings us to an important side note. Being part of the secret of the Lord does not mean losing your ability to use discernment when you speak.)

I have struggled with how much of this period of my life to share with you because I want to be an open book, but the sin of others involved in our story compels me instead to remain vague—to cover in silence. Suffice it to say that Bob and I had no masks on, and we met with some pharisaical spirits. Since that time, the Lord has brought much healing to those relationships. I have no doubt He desired for sin to be exposed and for us to walk in loneliness so we could learn about the secret of the Lord. Had we not walked in isolation, we could not have hungered for the great intimacy God promises in the body and learned to walk in it.

Can you think back to a deeply painful period in your life and place it right here in this chapter? Remember the fear of what others would think? The loneliness? The isolation? Oh, how you felt like quitting, huh? But God does not want us to quit. He desires for us to persevere.

The only way for me to do that was to cling to the many blessings I'd been living in since I'd taken my mask off. If God could use me after my teenage sexual sin, which was so much "bigger," then I knew He would use Bob and me yet again in spite of this place of repentance we were in. During this time of uncertainty, I feasted, not on the stories of others who'd lived in God's great adventure, but on the stories of adventure He'd been writing in *my* life.

For instance, I received a letter from a young reader who had gone through *And the Bride Wore White* with her church friends. Let me first tell you that one of the lessons I most love sharing with teen girls is how I was living like a trashable Styrofoam cup when I gave myself away sexually. And I got trashed. I encourage girls to step beyond even the world's casual lifestyle of being a ceramic mug to live before God a priceless, set-aside, valuable, untouched teacup. This precious writer tells me about another reader we'll call Amber, who'd been living as a ceramic mug:

> I wanted to share with you about one girl in particular. Amber. 13 years old, 8th grade, and led to Christ by [another girl in this study group]. Your words challenged Amber to live a life of purity. Little did we know, it was in preparation to see God. Amber also has a brother. December 21st he was playing with a gun. It accidentally went off and shot Amber. She died early December 22nd. Today, December 23rd, was her viewing. They had a table next to her coffin that had her school agenda, some pictures, etc. There was also a book, well read. Your book. Also, next to the guest book was a letter she had written to God at the beginning of your study. . . . I am telling you this so that you will know that your obedience to God has so richly blessed us. And thanks to your guidance, Amber left behind her ceramic mug and is now before God, a lovely, dainty tea cup. God bless you, Mrs. Dannah, for obeying Him when He told you to share your heart.

What a treasured letter. I cried many tears. Then I realized that as sad as this was, her parents themselves had to be celebrating at the wonderful way God prepared Amber in her last days to be pure and prepared to see Jesus. Then, as only we women can, I cried again. This time I released great tears of gratitude and joy that God used my life to touch Amber's. Celebrate with me! That's what the secret of the Lord does. We share the bad and the good! You've seen my sin and mourned; now rejoice with me that God has used it for His good.

What if Amber's Bible study friend had not feared God and shared Christ with her? What if I'd not feared God to write that first book? Oh, that I would operate in the fear of God more consistently.

The Fear of God Is Birthed by Repentance

Fearing God is the opposite of fearing man, but it is more than that. As I study the fear of God, it seems to me that it is brought forth by a thorough spirit of repentance. Psalm 130:3–4 says, "If you, O LORD, kept a record of sins, O LORD, who could stand? But with you there is forgiveness; *therefore* you are feared" (emphasis mine)! I believe such fear follows forgiveness at a deep level. Not your surface-sins forgiveness, but a truly repentant-to-the-core-of-our-being forgiveness.

We are a people hungry for the palpable presence of God. Today that comes in the form of His Holy Spirit. The first manifestation of the Spirit is always repentance. In John 16:8 Jesus is recorded as having said, "When he [the Holy Spirit] comes, he will convict the world of guilt in regard to sin and righteousness and judgment." If you are looking for the Holy Spirit, don't look for a hushed stillness or comforting prophecies or new languages or giggling with joy or even miracles. These things may or may not come. What you can be sure will come and what you should look for is repentance. That's what comes first.

We Need to Practice Alabaster Worship

Remember that sinner woman who poured her alabaster jar of ointment out on the feet of Jesus? We visited her story a few chapters ago. What caused that woman not to care what the Pharisees and others thought? What gave her courage to interrupt a dinner to which she was not invited to weep over and anoint her Savior's feet? In that culture, it was absolutely unheard of for a woman to touch a man in the way that she touched Christ. It was unacceptable on several levels. Why was she willing to do it anyway? Why did she not fear man that day?

> *"It was the act of a woman who had not been tamed by cynical religious attitudes. She came across those attitudes that day, but was unaffected by them. It was the worship of a woman who didn't know the rules—an unpredictable, untamed heart on a quest to see Jesus glorified."*[2]
>
> —Matt Redman
> on the sinner woman's alabaster jar in her worship of Christ

She poured her alabaster jar out on the feet of Jesus. This was no small thing. Many women of that time had alabastrons. These were tiny bottles made of clay or alabaster. The clay was obviously more common and less expensive. Hers was made of alabaster.

Women with less expensive jars had theirs filled with olive oil. Women with alabaster usually had theirs filled with something costly like spikenard, a rare perfume.

We can assume that hers was probably worth about 500 denarii, making it cost a full year's wages. What's that to you? $20,000? $50,000? $100,000? Would you "waste" it on worshipping Jesus?

The monetary value was nothing compared to the jar's intrinsic value. It was a kind of dowry. It was meant to be saved and poured on her groom's feet the night of their wedding. Without it, she had little hope of ever securing a husband. In the Middle East during the time of Christ, a woman's only perceived value was being a wife and bearing children. In pouring the contents of her alabaster jar onto Christ she was saying, "I have no future but You. I have no value but loving You. I am Yours."

What would cause her to throw her future away like that, and in front of those who disdained her for her sin? Repentance! A deep realization that she'd been forgiven of much! This woman saw her sin. She knew how unworthy of Christ's forgiveness she was, and because of that awareness, costly and unconditional love poured from her heart and from her jar.

In Luke 7:47, Jesus said that "her many sins have been forgiven—for she loved much. But he who has been forgiven little loves little." It doesn't say that those who've sinned much love much. It says those who've been forgiven much love much. I think the issue is not how much sin is in your life, but how much repentance there has been, giving way to forgiveness.

THE FEAR OF GOD FREES US FOR BIGGER DREAMS

When we repent of our sin, we are able to rise up to fear God rather than man. What follows are those wonderful blessings God promises to those who fear Him, including the intimacy that you and I are so craving in today's church experience. Those blessings give us courage to fear Him yet again when the enemy makes it even more difficult.

I believe that when I reached for this new dream for Africa, God needed me to weep over my sin once again. He needed to cleanse me to the very core so that I could truly love Him enough to begin to be released from my fear of man. Had I not endured that, I would not have had the conviction in my heart to obey God in the bigger, better dream He now has me living in.

THE FEAR OF GOD BRINGS REWARDS

I just have to share with you the vibrant fear of God that resides in a woman I know named Kristina. She's a vivacious singer and actress in her twenties. She has a smile that's contagious and a gift of evangelism like few I've seen.

Last summer she was in a wedding in the Midwest and showed up to find out that the bridal party's last-night fling was at a salsa bar. Salsa . . . not as in chips and salsa, but dancing! This precious woman of God sat there in that bar, getting propositions and feeling very out of place.

"God, why am I here?" she asked.

Immediately she felt led to invite the other bridesmaids and the bride to a challenge. "From now on, when someone asks us to dance, let's just say, 'I can't dance with you, but how can I pray for you?'" she asked sincerely and enthusiastically. "Let's just see what God does."

She was met with blank stares. Right about then, I'd be asking God for an easy way out. Something like, "Ah, excuse me, but I'm allergic to salsa!" Or "Wow, look at the time . . ." But Kristina had just been called to fear God. Soon, a guy who'd already hit on her came up to her and asked again if she would please dance with him.

"I can't dance with you, but how can I pray for you?" she asked with a smile.

The man was stunned. He broke. He explained that he'd left his wife and three children that morning and was contemplating divorce. Right there in the middle of the salsa bar, Kristina prayed for him and encouraged him. She invited him to go to church with her and her husband on Sunday and gave him her husband's cell phone number, uncertain as to whether she'd ever hear from him again.

Sunday morning as church was about to begin, the phone rang. "Ah, yeah," came an awkward voice. It was him! "I'm in this town, but I can't find that church you told me about."

Kristina gave him directions, and soon she and her husband met him at the door. The first worship song that morning was an upbeat song of praise, but when your need is great, any connection with God can cause you to crumble. And crumble he did. He had little composure through the service, and at the end he darted down the aisle to recommit his life to Christ. The pastor scheduled the first marriage counseling meeting for him and his wife that day.

That's what fearing God accomplishes!

Do you think that Kristina felt like ministering that night? Do you think that she felt like asking a guy if she could pray with him after the friends she was sitting with made it clear to her that they didn't like that idea? For her, it came down to simple, old-fashioned obedience that night. And the Spirit answered in the form of repentance in her new friend's life.

Simple acts of fearing Him result in wonderful rewards.

I knew that. I'd experienced it. I was clinging to it as I walked through a disapproving crowd trying to find the courage to keep fearing Him.

ALABASTER WORSHIP

My husband knows how I love this story of the sinner woman pouring out her life through her alabaster jar. So for Christmas last year, he searched and searched until he found an alabastron from 33 BC, which is very close to the time period of the story in Luke 7, so it may be somewhat like the alabaster jar she used. Knowing I might not recognize this antiquity when I saw it, he carefully gave me clues.

The first was some Dead Sea salts. I knew it was something of biblical value.

The next was a scroll with the Luke 7 passage written on it. "An alabaster jar!" I squealed, as I reached for the last box. I pulled an itty-bitty 3½-inch piece of aged marble from the box.

"Is this the lid?" I asked with delight, only to see my husband's face drop in disappointment.

"No, that's the whole jar," he reported.

It was so tiny. I never pictured it being so simple and so small. But sometimes that's all God wants. Small and simple acts of devotion. Our small acts of worship and obedience make a big difference to God. And they give us courage to obey Him in bigger ways.

ᐦ— It's Your Turn —ᐦ

What small act of worship can you pour upon Him today? Journal it out. Nothing like big trips to Turkey or Russia. No launching of international ministries (just yet)! What *little* act of fearing God will help you build confidence for bigger ones?

Have you a mean neighbor who needs a fresh-baked batch of your famous chocolate chip cookies? A boss who's contemplating divorce and needs a tender, humble word of truth? A husband who needs to hear you say, "I'm sorry" and mean it? A five-hundred-dollar bonus that's supposed to be poured out in ministry even though you'd rather pour it out at the mall? (OK, maybe that's not so small!) What small act of worship is God calling you to today?

PART FOUR

The Covenant

CHAPTER TEN

Yada! Yada! Yada!

Search me, O God, and know my heart.
—PSALM 139:23

I was losing hope.

I didn't feel released from my call, but as the months dragged on I felt less and less qualified. Any wide-eyed confidence that I could make a difference in Africa was gone. I clung to just a thread of faith.

"You did call me, didn't You, Lord?" I prayed.

I'd been asking for nearly a year that God would open the door. Almost to the day, I'd been in a place of painful refinement. Some days I was just certain I'd not heard God correctly. Pain does that. You begin to lose hope in the future and faith in, not God, but His desire to use you.

"Lord, I cannot go on any longer," I cried one Saturday afternoon as I curled into a ball and cried things out in my walk-in closet. "Are these people right? Am I unfit to serve You right now? Have I been foolish in thinking I have gifts You can use? Oh, Lord, many have suggested that my faith is not strong enough right now to serve You. Do You desire that I sit on the sidelines? If You do, I will."

As we drove to morning worship the next day, my mind suddenly seemed to be engulfed with a very specific and distinct question. "Honey," I asked Bob, "didn't you once say that Mr. Lehr spoke at the men's retreat about hearing from the Lord in dreams?"

"Yep," Bob answered.

I pictured Mr. Lehr. He was one of the greatest servants of God in my conservative, mainstream congregation. His was a quiet faith, marked by repairing metal folding chairs and hugging the children at their worship service. I remembered watching him sit in the same place Sunday after Sunday as I was growing up, and especially I remembered the evenings when he'd share how he'd witnessed to yet another life. Many hearts had come into the kingdom through his quiet obedience. His dreams intrigued me because he was a man of solid, quiet faith.

"I'd really like to hear about that," I said. "Do you think we could have him and his wife over for dinner sometime?"

"Plan it," he said.

At church that day I made a beeline for Mr. Lehr and abruptly asked, "Mr. Lehr, Bob told me about your testimony concerning receiving dreams from the Lord, and I'd really like to hear about them . . ."

I would have continued, but his face was clearly marked with . . . was it amazement, was it fear, or was it excitement? I wasn't sure, really. Maybe it was a mixture of all of these.

He simply said, "What makes you ask me that?"

"Well, I'm not exactly sure," I answered. "No specific reason, but I'd like to learn more about that kind of gifting."

He pulled a folded white paper from his pocket and pressed it into my hand.

"I don't usually see you in church since we attend different services," he said. "But last night the Lord gave me a dream about you. I told Him I would share it with you only if I saw you today."

We stood there, me nearly in tears. Both of us were quite mindful that there was another Presence hovering between us, connecting us. I was quite certain that whatever was on that paper was a direct word from God.

And, oh, what a loving word it was.

Tears come to my eyes even as I remember that moment. (And I'm editing this for about the third time. How good God is to keep this memory fresh and preciously filled with His presence.) This treasured piece of paper is here beside me. It's a private and holy love letter to me from my great Savior. Probably not nearly as thrilling to you as it was for me that day as I received it. Like a couple of girlfriends listening in while a friend "privately" reads a few lines from her fiancé's love letter, curl up with me and share the romance!

Dear Dannah,

I just had a dream. I believe many of my dreams are from the Lord, and this is one of them . . .

In my dream . . . I shared with you what a blessing you are to me because you display many of the gifts of the Spirit in your life . . . I even listed the gifts God blessed you with in order.

. . . Anyhow, that's the dream . . .

God asked Mr. Lehr, whom I don't know that well, to share specifically my spiritual gifts (something I felt very depleted of at the time). Visibly highlighted in the list of gifts is one I'd been painfully questioning if I even had or not. And get this, he concludes the letter saying he felt led to tell me to "continue to serve Him"!

Nothing could have ministered to my heart in quite the same way at that moment. How desperately I needed the evidence that God saw my hurt and doubt and that I was still chosen. I don't believe many of us enter into God's dream for our lives saying, "I'm so ready for this. I can't think of anyone more qualified." If we do, either we're tackling human-sized tasks, or we're so filled with pride we'll be of little use. When we follow God's dream for our lives, we need His reviving power.

KOINONIA

The secret of the Lord is a place of incredible intimacy. It is intimacy with God because we have intimacy with believers, and intimacy with believers because we have intimacy with God. They are like a circle, feeding one another. The writers of the New Testament often used the Greek term *koinonia* to describe this place. It meant "circle of friendship." It expressed fellowship, sharing, partnership. It speaks of being in the thick and thin . . . the profits and losses.

THE POWER TO SERVE

The lack of God's power in our lives isn't a result of not striving. If we do anything in our culture, we strive. We're busy. We often think being a part of the body of Christ requires us to jump into the rat race of Christian works, to say yes to every request the "church" makes of us. We feel guilty if we're not busy, busy, busy . . . but nothing could be a greater deception than thinking that busyness is what draws us close to God.

The famed Chinese evangelist Watchman Nee wrote,

Christianity does not begin with walking; it begins with sitting. Most Christians make the big mistake of trying to walk in order to be able to sit, but that is the reversal of the true order. Christianity is a queer business! If at the outset we try to do anything, we get nothing; if we seek to attain something, we miss everything. For Christianity begins not with a big DO, but with a big DONE![1]

What we have all too often today is rat-race Christians doing, doing, doing and never sitting in the presence of God. The power comes from simply being with Him. What happens when we are with Him? This is going to blow your mind! Do indulge me for a few moments while we seem to go off on a bunny trail. Let's talk about sex. (Hey! This is no ordinary bunny trail!)

Yada! Yada! Yada!

Check out Genesis 4:1. It says, "Adam lay with his wife Eve, and she became pregnant and gave birth to Cain." Adam lay. That word *lay* was the Hebrew word *yada*. (You'll never hear the saying "Yada! Yada! Yada!" the same way, will you?) *Yada* meant "to know, to be known, to be deeply respected." This word is used often throughout the Old Testament to describe the act of sexuality when it is between husband and wife and in the context of holy covenant. It speaks of a spiritual and emotional connection. It is the act of being naked emotionally and spiritually before a person. (No masks here!) It is the ultimate act of laying all your secrets out to be known. This word speaks of the emotional and spiritual passion that existed between Adam and Eve.

Sakab

Now, let's look to Genesis 19. Lot and his two daughters have just left Sodom for good. (Seeing as it's now a pile of ash!) Lot's wife's heart was all too tightly tangled into the sin of the city, and she, too, was permanently left behind, as a pillar of salt. Distraught and depressed, the daughters wonder how they will carry on the family name, having no brothers. The girls come up with a great idea . . . not! They decide to get their father drunk and have sex with him. Genesis 19:33 says, "The older daughter went in and lay with him." Sounds similar to Genesis 4:1, huh? But be warned, my friend, this is not *yada!* This time the world *lay* is *sakab*. This Hebrew word means "to exchange bodily emissions." It's talking solely of the physical and, I might add, it's a somewhat disgusting term. There's no emotion. No intimacy.

Not all sex is the same. Some is sex as God designed it, and it is deeply fulfilling. Other types of sex are far from God's intended use and are a mere exchanging of body fluids. Yuck!

"Yada" is an emotional and spiritual nakedness as well as a physical act. Bob truly knows me. He knows every ugly sin in my life, every hope and dream in my heart, every awkward social faux pas, what I laugh at, and what I cry about. He knows me spiritually, emotionally, and physically. What amazes me is that he still brags about me! My ears ring with joy to hear him speak about me. I have never known him to condemn me in front of others, only to lift me up.

Three years ago, after his gentle prodding about my sin of lying, I wrote him a letter, confessing that he had been correct. I felt God wanted me to go back over the ways I'd hurt our marital intimacy by communicating all too often with equivocations, exaggerations . . . lies. I confessed as many moments of untruth as I could remember, one by one. Man, was that an ugly letter! He wrote me back in a sweet spirit of forgiveness. His letter began, "I know your secrets . . ."

I know your secrets.

These words were sweeter to me than "I love you" at the moment, for he was saying his love transcended my sin. He sees me, all of me, and loves me in all fullness. *This* is "yada"! The ability for me to enter into our marriage bed fully known and still deeply respected frees me to fully enjoy our intimacy.

Know Him
Make Him Known

Here's where it gets really good. The word *yada* is used in another way throughout the Old Testament. And I do mean throughout! The word shows up nearly 900 times. Look at how it's used.

> "And the Lord said to Moses, '. . . I am pleased with you
> and I know [*yada*] you by name.'"
> —Exodus 33:17

"He knows [*yada*] the secrets of the heart."
—PSALM 44:21

"O LORD, you have searched me and you know [*yada*] me."
—PSALM 139:1

"Search me, O God, and know [*yada*] my heart."
—PSALM 139:23

"But I know [*yada*] where you stay and
when you come and go."
—ISAIAH 37:28

". . . you may know [*yada*] that I am the LORD,
the God of Israel."
—ISAIAH 45:3

See it?
Get it?
Know Him!
Know Him!
Know Him!
Do you know Him?

I can honestly say that when I was still wearing my mask ten years ago, I really thought I knew God. I didn't. Not intimately. Oh, I had a relationship with Him, and I was cracking my Bible for ten minutes a day, but I didn't recognize His voice as I did my lover's. I didn't know what it was like to feel His touch in my life. I didn't have a craving to be alone with Him. I didn't have a holy place that was just for Him and me.

Spiritually speaking, there is "yada" and there is a counterfeit like "sakab." We can go through a lot of similar motions to "know" God and all the while have nothing but a cheap imitation of the real intimacy He intended. It frightens me to the core when I realize that God says, "Depart from me. I never knew you" (see Matt. 7:23) to people who thought they were believers and who want to enter into His heaven. But in reality they were just going through the motions in a flurry of religious activity. He is very serious about our relationship with Him being authentic and intimate. No rat-race, routine Christianity. He wants us to know the real deal. What do you have? Something real? Yada? Or something far from satisfying because it's a fake?

When I realized I wanted . . . needed . . . couldn't live without a real, deep, intimate relationship with God, I made some changes. I started to reclaim my holy place by canceling power lunches. Time with Him had to be carved into my busy life. So instead of having lunch with business friends or clients, I headed out to the local community park and had lunch with God every day. If somehow that was impossible, I would hide away in a bubble bath after I put the kids to bed. But I was clearly staking my claim. I was going to get to intimately know my God.

When I laid the time aside, I changed. I was transformed as my mind was renewed by His Word and His presence. That gave me a new power in my life. My husband saw it. My mom saw it. Women and girls, suddenly and without explanation, sought my counsel, and I was able to lead them to Jesus or closer to Him. If there be any glory or praise, it is God's. I certainly had done a lot of striving before and had gotten nowhere. Now, with a "yada" relationship with Him, I was useful.

PERSONAL TRANSFORMATION

It seemed just about the time I was catching my stride, God allowed me to be refined and humbled. I was ministering to larger crowds. My first book hit the CBA bestseller list for the first time. And yes, pride was stepping my way. I was losing my focus. I wasn't resting in Him as I once did. And He let me hit a time of deep refinement, tenderly calling me back to rest more deeply. I suddenly had to make more changes. Take more bubble baths. Stake reclamation of my holy space. How tenderly He loved me during this difficult time. And I now know it was so that I could be used in a very specific way. (Gotta save that for later!)

BILLY GRAHAM'S YADA MOMENT

Billy Graham learned this the hard way. He had already begun his public ministry when he was called to Wales to preach the gospel. He recalls walking off the stage of a Youth for Christ rally after the third meeting and being very much aware that the crusade lacked something. But what was it? Attendance? Yes. That was obvious, but it was more. This crusade lacked power.

Graham sought mentoring for himself right away. He tracked down Steven Olford, an evangelist whom Graham felt had something more . . . something that Graham wanted. The two men sequestered themselves in a hotel room, where Olford first discipled Graham in the art of "quiet time." He urged Graham to develop a life of prayer and Bible study. Graham made a commitment to do so.

On the second day, Olford challenged the twenty-eight-year-old Graham to fully surrender himself to Christ anew in sustained prayer time. Olford began to pray for Graham. Billy prayed silently. After some time, he suddenly cried out, "Lord I will not let Thee go except Thou bless me." He then began fervently praying, pouring his heart out in total surrender to God. At a pivotal climax of prayer, he turned to Steven Olford and said, "My heart is so aflood with the Holy Spirit, I want to laugh and praise God all at the same time." He declared, "I have it. I'm filled!"

That night, the crusade hall was inexplicably filled to overflowing, and Billy Graham spoke with a new authority. Olford sensed something different. As soon as Graham gave an invitation to come forward, men and women flooded forward. And it became the pattern of his crusades.[2] (Would it be an appropriate time to remind us both that the first evidence of the Holy Spirit is repentance? When Billy Graham was touched by God's Spirit, the first evidence was the fruit of many coming to God in repentance when this dear man of God lifted up the Savior.)

> *"Once we see ourselves as sinners,*
> *we can stop trying to earn God's favor*
> *and learn to rest in God's arms."*[3]
> —MARK MCMINN

Billy Graham sat in the presence of God. He'd begun to know (*yada*) God. The fruit began to flood his life and has yet to cease.

Girl, we've got to stop thinking we can let dead works birthed from busyness reflect God. They're pitiful attempts to glorify Him. Instead, we've got to carve out a holy place of intimacy that's just for sharing with our beloved Savior. How beautiful that He gives us the portrait of Himself as our intimate Lover. Oh, let us enter into a holy place of satisfaction with Him.

In challenging teens to live lives of purity, my husband and I teach them about yada. Our slogan has become, "Know Him. Make Him known." The power to make Him known comes from simply knowing Him.

Slow down today.

Know Him.

Lexi's Yada Moment

A few summers ago, my sweet Lexi and I went through the mother/daughter devotional I've written called *Secret Keeper Girl*. During the study, we are both charged to an intimate twenty days of devotions. Lexi dug in with all her might, hearing from God in a powerful and unique way.

"Mom," she said to me one day. "You see that flag over there?" She pointed to a flag I was unfamiliar with. "I've seen it in a few places lately," she said. "And each time I do, I feel like God is telling me that I'm going to do something that has to do with that flag."

That's yada! Having been in deep fellowship with Him each day, she recognized His voice.

Weeks went by and we learned that the flag was the South Korean flag. Nothing really significant happened. We both just gave it to God.

In July of that summer, Lexi went to Camp K, our local Christian camp. There she met a girl named Hannah who became a new friend. On the last night of camp, Hannah was sitting next to Lexi at the bonfire, where the camp director encouraged campers who didn't know Jesus to begin that life-changing relationship. Lexi couldn't help herself. Something inside of her just rose up. She turned to Hannah in the middle of the service, and out of her mouth flowed wisdom.

"Hannah," she asked, "have you ever asked Jesus into your heart?"

Tears began to flow from Hannah's eyes. She had reservations. A Bible verse popped out of Lexi's mouth. She would later say, "Mom, I didn't even know I knew that verse, but it was just what she needed to hear."

Moments later, Lexi led her first soul into the kingdom of God.

One week later, Hannah returned to her home country. South Korea.

That's yada!

∾— It's Your Turn —∾

Make a specific commitment today to reclaim that holy place for you and God. It seems to me that the best way to do this is to just enjoy Him. If you make it a duty to come before Him, you are really exalting yourself above God and making Him the one who benefits from your precious time. So, today throw that journal aside and rush to the great outdoors. Find a sparkling brook to sing to you, a sunset to memorize, some flowers to smell, or a grassy bed to lie in. Just be with Him. Don't stop until you've felt His presence. If you need to cry, cry. If you feel like laughing, laugh. If you need to rest, rest. But do it with Him. Like two lovers who don't necessarily need to talk to communicate . . . just be with Him. Know Him. Yada Him!

CHAPTER ELEVEN

Covenant Power

And these signs will accompany those who believe: In my name they will drive out demons; they will speak in new tongues; they will pick up snakes with their hands; and when they drink deadly poison, it will not hurt them at all; they will place their hands on sick people, and they will get well.

—MARK 16:17–18

It had been one and a half years. For eighteen months, I'd been quietly asking God to open our own special door to Africa. I still knew no one there.

I looked out at the soft December snow blanketing the mountain above Happy Valley. "Release us in December," I read from my journal. I'd written it sixteen months ago, pleading with God that the full release from our hurt and the open door to our calling would become visible. It hadn't. December had come and gone. We'd arrived at yet another.

I stumbled over to my computer to check my e-mail. One stuck out from the others. It read:

> Dear friends of abstinence,
>
> Greetings in the wonderful name of our Lord and Savior

*JESUS CHRIST. My name is John Banda . . . We have been
authorized by the government of the Republic of Zambia . . . to
conduct the abstinence education curriculum for 73 government schools. We will be presenting this curriculum to over
100,000 . . . We need you to train these 30 volunteers for five
days . . . We trust our appeal finds favour with you . . .*

In His Service
"John"

There in my little home office, I actually looked over my shoulder
as if Someone had just pointed to me and I was certain He was pointing at the person behind me. There was no one there. It was for me. It
was my call.

One month later a small handful of friends had collected nearly
$10,000 to make the trip possible for us.

Two months later, we began our research.

Three months later, we had a one-week curriculum written and
the materials collected for our already beloved students.

Four months later, we were on a plane to Zambia, Africa, for the
adventure of our lives.

Yes, my friend, it is often in our season of resting and "knowing
Him" that we find our greatest calling. Rest. That is the place of His
reviving power. We all too often think we'll find power in our
busyness. We don't. That's a great deception. It's a deception built
upon good works. While many of us can never imagine being good
enough to earn our way into heaven, we often live as if that is what
we believe. Nope! That's not where the power is to be found.

The core to this power that God promises to you and to me is found in something called "covenant." Our special verse tells us, "The secret of the LORD is with them that fear him, and he will shew them his *covenant*."

I cringe to hear this precious word—*covenant*—thrown around almost as if it is just slightly more binding than a contract or an agreement. It is so much more than that. And, if you'll explore it with me, you'll begin to see the pathway through which we are able to live in true power.

Let's start with a few familiar names we find in the Old Testament. These guys understood covenant.

A COVENANT IS AN UNBREAKABLE BOND

A covenant has no nonbinding loopholes. It has no clauses that enable the parties to be released. Covenants are unbreakable.

God's Old Testament covenant was made with an old man named Abram. He was well into his eighties and, still, he and his wife Sarai had no children. But God, in His ever-amazing way of showing His power through our weaknesses, chose this well-worn man. For what? To begin a long line of descendants that He will love in a way like no other people to walk the earth. To bring forth through natural birth "His people."

Guess what happens when this man and God enter into covenant? Abram's name changes! Abram becomes known as Abraham. God even changes Sarai to Sarah. Some Bible scholars have suggested that God was taking the "H" from his own Hebrew name, "Yahweh" or "YHWH" and placing it within their names.[1]

Why? So that they will be forever branded, marked, recognized, and known to be in relationship with Him.

God even changes His own name. From that point on, He often calls Himself "the God of Abraham." Others refer to Him in that way. We still refer to Him as the "God of Abraham, Isaac, and Jacob," those who were eventually born out of this once barren couple's moment of "yada."

God and Abraham are forever marked as belonging to each other. A covenant does that. It binds you to the point of being inseparable.

You and I are not under this old covenant, but under what Jesus referred to as the "new covenant." As such, we are called to bear His name. I believe this is why it is so vital that we overcome the fear of man to unashamedly "wear" the name of Jesus Christ at every moment of our lives. We are forever His!

A Covenant Is Sealed in Blood

Abraham is called by the Lord to seal the covenant in blood through animal sacrifice. There was a high price paid for covenant in the Old Testament. Life. An animal had to be carved in two. The Old Testament word for covenant was *beriyth*, which meant "to pass between flesh." Abraham was called to cut the animals sacrificed into halves and to literally walk between the pieces of meat in the blood of the animals. Without this blood there was no covenant.

Can you imagine how that moment felt? Abraham was personally selected by God to be the seed maker of His treasured people. What a moment of "yada" that must have been, but Abraham, as we often do, falters as the tenderness of that moment fades into the past. He still believes he is the seed maker, but he decides to take matters into his own hands. He takes Sarah's handmaid, Hagar, and has sex with her. The result is a son who was *not* the seed of the covenant. Abraham sinned. But he is extended a second chance.

This time, God wants Abraham to "get it." So He asks for blood yet again . . . this time from the site of paternity. Ya know what I'm sayin'? I mean, let's be ladies here but be clear that God is calling for the blood to come from this man's most tender spot. Circumcision is still widely practiced today as a medical intervention against disease, but it was originally "invented" by God as a method of sealing His covenant in blood.

What do you think that old man did? Well, he circumcised himself and his entire household that very night! Wouldn't you think he'd wait awhile and hope God could be kidding? No, because this man lived in a day and age when he knew the power of the blood. There was no covenant without it. And he wasn't about to miss this second chance.

Today, we do not have to practice such bloody things to be in covenant with God. Jesus Himself states in Matthew 26:27–28, Mark 14:24, and Luke 22:20 that His own life brings us the blood of the new covenant. It is His free gift to us. It comes at no cost to us, unlike Abraham's covenants. We must simply embrace it.

A Covenant Has Requirements and Blessings

Abraham lived under a heavy covenant. He had lists and lists of laws to live under. The faith of Old Testament believers was built upon routine and steady observance of many, many rules. But it was worth it. In turn, God protected His people. He often did this supernaturally, exemplifying His ownership over these people. He used earthquakes. He turned bodies of water to blood. He opened rivers up and made them wide and dry for His people. He rained manna from heaven. He ignited water-saturated altars of wood with fire from heaven. He made Himself known through wonders and signs.

His covenant promises that He will still do this for you and me today. You and I have not so many rules to live under. While God offers us many suggestions and commandments for living a happier and scar-free life, He gives us His salvation as a free gift. However, there's still one thing He calls us to in order to see those signs and wonders. It's found in the Great Commission. Mark 16:15–18 tells us that this covenant requires us to "go into all the world and preach the good news" and to baptize people in His name.

In turn, He promises that we will heal the sick, drive out demons, speak in new tongues, pick up snakes and not be harmed, and drink poison and live. In Matthew 28:20, He also promises that He will be with us to the very end of the age. The Mark passage has been highly criticized or even explained away. For example, some commentaries say the passage about the serpents wasn't really about being able to be bitten by a snake and live. (Then why is it that this actually happened to the apostle Paul?) They reason that this is probably just a figurative reference to the serpent we know as the devil. (I guess, then, I would ask what is more miraculous—that we would overcome an earthly snake or Satan?) I haven't even gotten to the tongues or poison yet!

We can get into semantics if you want, but I think the bottom line is that we find an amazing if/then agreement in both of these passages. If we are faithful to spread the gospel, then we will see wondrous things. No one really criticizes Matthew's recorded promise that if we are faithful to spread the gospel, then God will be with us to the end of the earth. Is there anything more amazing than this? That God would dwell with us who were once separated from Him? The bottom line is that covenants promise blessings. The covenant of the cross extends the blessings of forgiveness and eternal life as well as abundant, miraculous power.

THE COVENANT HAS POWER

My brother, Darin, is a living miracle. When he was a baby, he lay dying in a hospital bed. He was just a few months old and was literally in a coma. A pastor came to visit my mother, Kay, as she was in shock from the doctor's request to prepare for the worst. This dear pastor, Raymond Dibble, explained that he didn't know if God would heal her baby, but he knew God wanted to heal her heart. He explained to her the simple plan God has given to us through Jesus Christ for eternal life. And she accepted the free gift of forgiveness.

That's when the miracle began. That night she lay stroking her precious son, unwilling to say good-bye. She lifted a simple, untrained prayer. "God, I will serve You if You heal my baby. Give me faith to believe You will." At that moment, the little guy woke up, lifted his head, and smiled at his mama. He then quickly returned to his coma.

My mother was wild with faith. (I love that about new believers!)

"Jesus has healed my baby," she told the doctors, who kindly explained she should not get her hopes up. A few days later when Darin awakened, they continued to attempt to squelch her faith, explaining that he'd be a "vegetable" his whole life due to the length of time his brain was shut down.

"Jesus has healed my baby," she responded.

A few days later, when he began to move around and later when he began to crawl, they explained to her that he would most likely never speak due to extreme brain trauma.

"Jesus has healed my baby," she said for nearly three years, during which time Darin did not speak. One day she was exasperated by his pointing and told him she would not give him the cereal he wanted unless he asked for it. He did . . . in a complete sentence.

Of course, then the doctors explained that he'd be mentally challenged and would need special schooling.

"Jesus has healed my baby," she said, even through all of kindergarten where Darin was socially shy and the schools wanted to hold him back. My mother believed and prayed . . . and enrolled him in a new private Christian school where Darin was tested and accepted into first grade. By seventh grade, he was doing college-level math.

He is our family's living sign and wonder!

We want the signs and wonders. We want to be healed from depression. We want to see our loved ones overcome addictions. We desire those friends who are dying to be supernaturally healed. We want the power, but are we willing to live under the obligations of this covenant to see them? Are we willing to share the story of Jesus' salvation over and over and over again with no fear of what others will think? Until we are, I fear we will see little power.

SHARE THE GOSPEL

Even into the beginning of my ministry, I was unlikely to share the gospel. I knew it needed to be shared with my audiences at retreats as they grew into larger crowds of two hundred, five hundred, or a thousand teenagers, but I was afraid to share it myself. I assigned it to other team members. I was afraid!

But as I came to understand that this fear of man was a sin and that the power of God was linked to my obedience in sharing the Great Commission, my tongue began to become hot with passion to share.

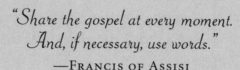

"Share the gospel at every moment.
And, if necessary, use words."
—FRANCIS OF ASSISI

A college girl named Katie, with a heart bloodied and broken by sexual sin, sent an e-mail to me. She had just broken up with her boyfriend and wanted to know where to go for healing. Since she lived nearby, I suggested we meet. Understand, her e-mail described an active church member, and so I easily assumed she was a Christian. It made absolutely no logical sense, but as I sat with her that evening, I felt compelled to open my Bible to John 3 and read the story of Nicodemus to her. I hesitated, feeling foolish. Wasn't this girl a believer already? But I was hearing my Savior's voice. I knew (*yada*) it. So I could trust it. I explained to Katie that though Nicodemus had spent his life as a religious man, he still didn't have a relationship with Jesus. That night, thanks to my new obedience to the Great Commission, Katie left with a new relationship with Jesus. The last I heard, she was helping to plant a new congregation in a very needy area in Pennsylvania.

Please understand. I'm as frightened as you are of the Great Commission. I still shake in my shoes every time I feel prompted to share. I really don't want to do it most of the time. I am scared silly every time God asks me to open my mouth. I realize that's only the enemy rearing his ugly head. That's his favorite way to show up. More than he likes to show up in shadowy figures, or foaming-at-the-mouth possessions, he just likes to make you and me cower when it comes to witnessing. It is at that moment that we choose whom we will submit to, stand in awe of, bow before, and worship. God or man.

Today's congregational paradigms don't really encourage us to open our mouths and testify. We wear ourselves out all too often on lots of programs and special events. We talk a lot about being "seeker friendly." *What's that?* Do you think that the Christian faith is seeker friendly in China, where the church is growing more rapidly than anywhere else on the globe, but believers have to hide in homes to fellowship? Come on! I know that we must be sensitive to cultural needs, fears, myths, and traditions in order to carry the message effectively, but the bottom line is that we need to just open up our mouths and speak it out!

Sometimes we won't be called to share the story of Nicodemus or the "Roman's road" or even to offer the precious gift of salvation, but we'll be called to simply live out our faith authentically. As I overcome my fear of man (and I've got a long way to go), I find myself realizing that sometimes I just have to live it, not speak it.

A few weeks ago, I was on a catamaran sailboat off of Key West. My family and I were seeking a snorkeling adventure, along with about fifty other vacationers. It was a bad day for snorkeling and for sailing. The ocean was rocky. All over the boat women were . . . well, how do I make this ladylike? I can't. It was gross. Terribly gross. Women were barfing. Seasickness is horrible! Just as one of them bent over the edge of the deck, I felt God's gentle nudging.

"Offer to pray for her," I felt Him say.

Now, you know I didn't come up with that one by myself. I reasoned. I tried to get out of it, but it was from God. Who was I going to bow to, God or man?

"Lord," I prayed, "do You want me to pray with that woman? If You do, please help me to do it without being forceful and insensitive to how horrible she feels right now."

Instantly, I realized I had a box of Dramamine (the reason I wasn't joining this sad club of the seasick)! I walked up to the woman and offered her a pill. She was very grateful. Then I simply asked, "Would you like me to pray for you, too?"

"Would you, please?" she pleaded.

I placed my hand on her back and simply prayed, "Lord Jesus, calm Stacey's body. Comfort her and let her feel better. In Your name, Amen!"

Not forced. Not awkward. Not big. Not self-righteous. Just kind.

Before I knew it, I was praying with another woman. I prayed with women until my box of Dramamine was empty. I may never know what seeds the Holy Spirit was able to plop into one of those lives that day, but I'm certain He will use that simple act.

Speak it out. Live it out. But let's stop wimping out! Join me in my quest to be an authentic Great Commission believer, leading others to Christ and discipleship.

STOP PLAYING CHURCH

In China, the house church movement has been instrumental in bringing many into relationship with Jesus Christ. Brother Yun, one of the movement's leaders, has not been concerned with a lot of programs and plans. He just obeys God, going wherever he's told, even jail, to open his mouth for Christ. In turn, he reports that signs and miracles are common. Of the Western church he says, "Until . . . the Great Commission is obeyed" we are "just playing with God."[2]

Erlo Stegan, a South African pastor I respect and admire, has prayed for the blind and they see, and prayed for AIDS patients and they are healed. He calls failing to live as Great Commission believers "playing church." He does not seek the signs and wonders. He seeks repentance for sin. Sometimes the signs and wonders follow. He often chastises his audiences, pleading, "Stop playing church." When he first yielded to God's call on his life, he said, "I don't want to be a preacher who entertains people on Sundays for an hour or two, who just baptizes, marries, and buries them. That isn't enough. I don't want to play church."[3]

Let's be honest. Here in the West, aren't we often just playing church? Let's not any longer. Let's *be* the church. Do you want to see God's signs and miracles happening as I do? Then, let us begin to obey the Great Commission. If we open our mouths and share the good news and baptize believers, signs and wonders will follow. The most powerful of these signs will be transformed lives.

"But," you might say, "I'm just one woman."

Did you know that most of the seven hundred pastors at the largest church in South Korea are women? Eighty percent of the house churches in China are led by women.[4]

Just one woman?

Did you know that Jesus first appeared to just one woman? Mary Magdalene was the first to carry the gospel message.

Just one woman?

Did you know that one of four women in the world is Muslim? Given the cultural restrictions, I doubt men will reach these precious women for Christ.

Just one woman?

That sounds just perfect to me. Why don't you start with reaching just one woman?

MORE ON COVENANT

This chapter just dips our proverbial toe into the concept of covenant. Two books I love that explore it more thoroughly are *Our Covenant God* by Kay Arthur and *The Lost Secret of the New Covenant* by Malcolm Smith.

᧬— It's Your Turn —᧬

Today, I want you to open your journal and close your eyes. Sit there, pen in hand, and ask the Lord whom does he desire you to bring into His family. With whom does He want you to share your faith? As names come to mind, write them down. Allow Him to bring to you names that are not obvious, such as "the mail carrier" or "my daughter's teacher." Begin to journal your feelings about being called to share Christ's salvation with them, and watch for the moment to do it. Don't let the fear of man engulf you. As one who's struggled very much, let me tell you, the only way to bust down that wall of fear is to run through it. Charge through it. But let me promise you this, until you begin to submit to the covenant requirements, you really are not going to live in the covenant power.

Try to reach just one woman today.

PART FIVE

Sharing the Secret

Chapter Twelve

The Hem of His Garment

When she heard about Jesus, she came up behind him in the crowd and touched his cloak, because she thought, "If I just touch his clothes, I will be healed." Immediately her bleeding stopped and she felt in her body that she was freed from her suffering.

—MARK 5:27–29

Oh, how we grew to love the people of Zambia in just a few days. Our core teaching, after months of craving this trip to Africa, was "the secret of the Lord." We wanted to encourage these people to take off their masks of perfection. In Africa, though HIV/AIDS consumes up to 50 percent of the population in some countries, it is still not something that people talk about openly. Rather, they slap on masks to hide their shame. This is especially true of people involved in any Christian church. If a person is found to have HIV/AIDS, it is not uncommon for him or her to be disciplined by being removed from church. Families will often shun those who've fallen to the disease. It does not matter whether sin is involved or whether the disease was acquired through rape or incest. Excommunication is the natural reaction.

Getting these Zambians to take off their masks was proving to be much more challenging than we'd anticipated. In the first four days of training, not one person had confessed in front of the others to having HIV/AIDS. The statistics betrayed their perfection. We knew in a group as large as the 30 students and 100 pastors we were training, this killer had certainly touched many lives.

One precious one came to us in private. I'll call her Elizabeth.

"I tested positive," she wept as she told me. The loneliness etched into her face was haunting. "I cannot tell anyone, or I will be kicked out of my church. My family doesn't know. They may disown me."

She felt so alone.

Her sadness instilled in me an even greater passion to see the secret of the Lord released in Zambia.

Later, as I stood before our little band of students, I asked, "Is it true that doctors sign death certificates that list the cause of death as TB or malaria when it is, in fact, AIDS that has ultimately led to death?"

"Yes," they answered in unison.

"Is it true that leaders in the church with HIV/AIDS will hide it so they are not disciplined with excommunication even though the sin may have occurred years and years ago?" I asked.

"Yes," they answered.

"Is it true that your youth don't believe anyone close to them has HIV/AIDS even though roughly 16 percent of this nation's population has it?" I asked.

"Yes," they answered.

"Is it true that fathers will rape their baby girls at the directive of the witch doctors who promise healing from the virus for such sin, but the family will hide this horrid act?" I asked.

"Yes," they answered.

"Do you understand that those struggling with sexual sin would never confess it to you because they've seen secrecy modeled all their lives?" I asked.

"Yes," they answered.

"Then how can you not speak out in truth? How can you not take off your masks of perfection? Until you do, you are only empowering the HIV/AIDS and the sin that leads to it."

They sat silently.

My heart was weary with effort. None of them was willing to share with the group that he or she had HIV/AIDS or even that anyone he or she loved had it.

"Isn't this why You brought us here, Lord?" I asked. "Isn't that why You gave us the message of the secret of the Lord? What are we doing wrong? Oh God, can You not unleash Your healing power through confession in this place?"

A few more came to us in quiet moments to privately confess their shame. They were so lonely. They described their pain so eloquently. Talked of being in darkness. Of having no one to talk to. Of the condemning tongues that chased them into deeper places of shame.

Only a person who has known this place of loneliness can recognize it. Bob and I recognized their pain from that place that was still fresh in our own hearts. I was beginning to realize that it was no mistake that God had taken us to that place. After nearly two years, God was about to show me why I had been returned to a place of loneliness.

I did not realize that the Lord was using our time of pain to prepare me for Africa. It didn't feel like preparation. It felt like an obstacle. I never doubted I would go someday, but conventional wisdom said, "Girl, your life is a mess. Don't complicate it any further by planning a missions trip you can't afford, to a country where you know not a soul and have not a single rational reason to be there!"

What did God need to teach Bob and me? He needed to teach us about the secret of the Lord. When we were the most unlovable . . .

. . . when we had no love to give out . . .

. . . when sin seemed to be the featured view . . .

. . . we found the secret of the Lord.

Don and Sarah and Jonathan and Suzy warmly and protectively flanked us in church during our deepest moments of despair and confusion. Dennis, who owns a successful business and is very busy, would come to sit with Bob on any and every whim. Rick and Ramona showed up in the middle of nowhere to spend a weekend soothing our hearts. Lynn would clear her busy schedule to meet with me, buy flowers with me, get massages with me, and just play with me in between deep conversations and heavy sessions of prayer. I sit here with tears flowing from my eyes, remembering these tender, indescribable moments of love. These busy, driven believers *spent* their lives on us. They allowed their time to be consumed by our hurt and pain.

They were the precious secret of the Lord.

God's Word says that they'll know we are Christians by our love (John 13:35). Remember that the covenant means we bear the image of Christ? Well, He Himself said that the greatest mark on us as believers would be our love. I'm not talking "country club" Christianity "love" where we hang together at Christmas musicals, church potlucks, and Wednesday night kids' ministry! I'm talking "yada" kind of love. I'm talking about being crazy lovers of God who lavishly spend time to know and be known. To share hopes, dreams, successes, fears, failures, and sin. Expressing love as the secret of the Lord is costly, and it will look different from the rest of the world's superficial love.

In going through this experience of discovering intimacy, God has unleashed a new power in my life . . . and in my husband's. This new power was one that God knew we would need in Africa. I would go through that period of pain again to have this gift that God has given to us.

Here's where we meet an important aspect of the secret of the Lord. It cannot be limited to our personal experience of church or God. It never looks the same from one place to another. The intimacy looks different from Africa to China to America to England to South Korea. It's achieved for different reasons and in different ways. The steps that lead up to experiencing this place of intimacy and power look different, too. The verse we've been studying points to three vital components: intimacy (the secret of the Lord), repentance (fearing God), and evangelism (the covenant). Beyond that, the manifestation of God's power differs from place to place.

Getting Close to Him

Let's look to a woman who knew His power, as recorded in Mark 5:21–34. As Jesus is walking along in the crowd, which is made up of people craving His power, something happens. A woman who has been bleeding for twelve years is in the crowd. She's obviously tried everything she possibly can think of for healing, but nothing has worked. Now desperate, she comes up behind Jesus, reaches low to the ground, and grasps the hem of Christ's garment, and suddenly, she is healed. The power is released. The bleeding stops.

Jesus actually stops because He knows that power has gone out from Him. The woman trembles and falls at His feet, confessing that she was the one who touched Him and that she is healed!

Bible commentaries, including *The Fourfold Gospel* and *Commentary Critical and Explanatory on the Whole Bible*, suggest that people started following this woman's example. They were crazy for the power of healing that she'd experienced. They knew how she got it, and so they thought they'd give it a try. They'd sneak up on the crowd and slide under it to grasp the hem of Christ's garment. In fact, many *were* healed in this way. "All who touched him were healed," records Matthew 14:36 as well as a similar passage in the Gospel of Mark.

Yet Christ varied His method of healing. Sometimes He simply touched the eyes of the blind, and their sight was restored. In Mark 8, Jesus spit on a man's eyes to heal him. And blind Bartimaeus received his sight when Jesus spoke, "Go, your faith has healed you" (Mark 10:52). This kind of variety in all of His healings is recorded throughout Scripture. Jesus didn't stick to one form of miracle but searched the hearts and minds of those He was about to heal to find the manner most appropriate for them.

In the story of the woman who touched the hem of Christ's garment, Jesus is actually on His way to Jairus's daughter, but by the time He arrives at their home, the child is dead. To Jesus, who understands that death is more about spiritual truth and not nearly so much about this physical realm, she is not dead but merely asleep. This brings us to the powerful conviction of the story. The next verse reads, "But they laughed at him" (Mark 5:40). Jesus has miraculously and through various means healed the multitudes, but here the crowd laughs at Him.

These stories provide such a profound picture of the modern church. We follow the plans and formulas of everyone else. We hear that this church found the power in small groups, so we rush to form some of our own but decide they are only a passing fad. It's said that that church found the power through Tuesday night prayer meetings, so we switch our prayer meetings to Tuesday night only to find them as quiet and uneventful as ever. Another church reports that studying a new method of evangelism did it for them. Still another has reports of ultraexperiential touches from God. We grasp after them all. We're just like those power-crazed people touching the hem of Christ's garment. And in many cases, we do find the same power others have found.

But often, if we're really truthful, we're all too much like the crowd at Jairus's house when something new comes along. Oh, I have been in that crowd! I am ashamed to admit it, but I have been the one to raise an eyebrow when I hear of another believer in Christ pursuing Him with something new and fresh. Can you admit with me that we, as a church, do this? Sadly, while we're questioning one innocent heart's attempt to reach Christ in a new way, we're busily trying to touch that same old place with which everyone else is familiar and comfortable.

Oh, that I would be more like the woman who reached for the hem of Christ's garment and less like the crowd at Jairus's home. I want to be the first to experience such power. How much power? The passage reads that she "touched" the hem of Christ's garment. The Greek word used there was *hapto,* and it means "to touch, hold, handle; to start a fire." Wow! I don't know about you, but I'd love to touch the fire of Christ's healing—not in my body only, but especially in my spirit.

BUILDING UNITY

This brings me to something I want to share tenderly. Let me first say that in traveling through the United States and ministering in nearly every different "brand" of Christian church, I've come to love the strengths of each denomination. Some are beautiful students of God's Word. Others are filled with awe, wonder, and respect for God, and I love the reverence with which they approach Him. Still others are very obedient to the presence of God and easily hear His voice. There are others who rise up to embrace world missions. If I've learned anything, I've learned that in our hearts we are all the same, and the strengths, if shared, would blow this world away. I love the church. I love the arms, the legs, the hands, the feet, the eyes. I love each part!

However, I fear that denominations are one of the greatest barriers to intimacy in the body of Christ. Denominational preferences are often the catalyst that causes our laughter to reflect the attitude of the crowd at Jairus's house. Let's be honest. We often fight over differences in worship and expressions of living out our faith in a way that is childish and worldly.

This is not happening in the countries where believers are persecuted or face other kinds of hardships. Instead, believers in China, South Korea, and Africa tend to be blind to denominations and doctrinal differences. They're just united by the cross of Christ and fulfilling His Great Commission. This gives them an odd freedom to experience Him in ways that are new and different to them . . . to be the first to touch the hem of His garment.

We cannot say that God "always" moves in a certain way. We cannot box God, and we cannot presume to know where His power will come from next. But let us never stop seeking intimacy, yada, in the body and with Him . . . for then we will never miss the new way in which He is going to move in our lives.

> *"The treacherous enemy facing the church . . .*
> *is the dictator of routine."*[1]
> —A. W. Tozer

There are times when His touch results in a miracle or an overflow of financial provision. There are times when it comes in emotional moments of healing or an unmistakable open door to serve Him. There are also times when He moves in ways that slow us down and let us hurt. I believe He desires far more to touch the broken parts of our soul than to give us money or stronger bodies. He wants our spirits to be strong.

I think of how His first amazing move in the apostle Paul's life was to strike him with blindness. What a painful way to "touch" the fire of God's power. And yet . . . what results! This period of pain prepared Paul to be a mighty servant of God.

In my life, God desired to move powerfully into my heart through deep pain as Bob and I discovered the secret of the Lord in our own circle of friends. Our pain was the door that opened up God's power in Ndola, Zambia. We were just about to "touch" it!

✑— IT'S YOUR TURN —✑

I think this is a good time to confess how you have judged other denominations or other Christians. Not ready to do that? Hmmmm, maybe *that's* what you should confess. I am thoroughly convinced that the secret of the Lord isn't something that you experience only within your little intimate small group or congregation. While it is in this place that it will be experienced most powerfully, we are called to have the hope of such intimacy with the universal church. Perhaps it is time to overcome our fear of man to obey the words of Jesus when He says that the second greatest commandment is to love one another. Would you take some time in your journal to confess specifically a way you have judged a believer or group of believers who've experienced God's power and presence in a way that you have not?

CHAPTER THIRTEEN

Walking with the Maskless

> Brothers, if someone is caught in a sin, you who are
> spiritual should restore him gently. But watch yourself, or
> you also may be tempted.
>
> —GALATIANS 6:1

*I*t was Friday. Our last day with these new friends.

I sat on a crude wooden bench in a dirt-floored mission station as Bob rose to address these precious pastors and church leaders. He set his notes aside, and I watched as he spent nearly two hours unfolding a deep teaching on grace versus ungrace. He asked them if their response to victims of HIV/AIDS was one of grace or ungrace. They wanted to have grace, but not to extend it. They wanted to reserve certain sins for permanent disqualification in church service and membership.

In exasperation Bob asked, "OK, I want you to name the sins that are not deserving of grace."

They did. Specific sins. One by one. And finally . . . a familiar one.

One that created the catalyst to send us running into our recent time of hiding.

Suddenly, the look on Bob's face changed. I could see him processing and weighing something in his mind.

"I want to tell you something I have never spoken of in public," he said with a new confidence and boldness. "I want to confess to you a moment of sin in my life . . ."

He went on to share in detail the sin he'd allowed to overcome him just two years before. He took off his mask.

He paused as tears welled in his eyes.

"I hate my sin," he confessed, punctuating each word with certainty.

The energy in the debate fizzled. The room was silent. Then, knowing that he loved them and they had learned to love him, he went out on a limb. "Am I disqualified from teaching you today?" he humbly asked.

Something broke.

First one began weeping. Then another. Within minutes the entire room was on the floor, faces before God, weeping in repentance. They pleaded out loud for God to forgive them for being a church that lacked grace.

It was musical. Heartfelt prayers rose amid brokenness and weeping. All expressed themselves before God in their own unique ways. None were silent.

Moments later a handsome young church leader ironically named Wisdom bravely hobbled to the front. He shared a beautiful and anointed confession of past sexual sin and the consequences of it. He said that he'd been in a place of purity for many years and wanted very much to receive grace from the body of Christ.

Suddenly, he stood silently. The room was hushed.

"I have HIV," Wisdom confessed.

His mask crashed to the floor, breaking into thousands of pieces.

"We didn't know it until a small sore on my leg would not heal. It just grew and grew and grew. None of the doctors understood why. Until I took a blood test and they realized it was because of HIV that my simple wound would not heal," he said, raising his pant leg to reveal a pole where a leg should have been. "This is the consequence of my moments of selfish sin."

There was an awkward pause. I walked over and placed my arms around him, feeling the frailty of his thin body. Silently, Bob joined me, flanking Wisdom on the other side.

I did not know what would happen next. Would this band of pastors, leaders, and church members, who moments ago were crying for discipline no matter what, be moved to extend grace?

We waited. There was a short awkward pause. Suddenly, almost all at once, the pastors and leaders began to rise. One by one they gathered around this dear maskless one and lifted him up in prayer.

What heavenly prayers they were. What healing permeated the air.

Hours later, as we all reluctantly left that place, I looked over to see Wisdom with his hands on the shoulders of another. This time he was praying for someone. Who was that? As her face turned, I saw her. It was Elizabeth.

She finally had someone to tell.

She was no longer alone. The silence was broken by a story. A simple story.

Our team of Zambian teachers is still working to get out the message of purity and hope and healing from AIDS. Wisdom's story opened up their hearts and their mouths. The very next day

Wisdom shared his story in front of about one hundred teens. Within a few days, others were telling their stories. My heart breaks when I hear them.

A precious young girl recently confessed that her father had been having sex with her. His witch doctor told him he should do this so he could be "cured of HIV/AIDS." After each encounter, he poured melted plastic over her arms and told her that what he would do to her would be much worse if she ever told anyone. But she met our team. They had the secret. And she found help and hope in the reviving power of the secret of the Lord. She found people who were willing to walk with her.

Don't be too quick to judge our Zambian brothers and sisters. We in the Western church are not free from shunning those who sin. I see it all too often.

WALK BESIDE THE BROKEN

Galatians 6:1 says, "Brothers, if someone is caught in a sin, you who are spiritual should restore him gently." The Greek word for "restore" was a medical term used for the process of taking a dislocated bone and resetting it into its proper position. The next time you know of a brother or sister who is facing his or her own sin, remember that you are called to reset this brokenness into a proper position of purpose! Never does a believer need more help re-dreaming than when faced with one's own human bent to fail. Oh, my friend, walk with the broken.

A few years ago I received an e-mail from a woman whose college-aged daughter had found the man she believed she would marry. As the couple's engagement became imminent, the young woman confessed to past sexual sin of which she was deeply ashamed. After consulting with his father, the young man returned her humble confession with one sad statement, "I forgive you, but I can no longer marry you." He walked away. The mother and daughter together were crushed. Dreams splattered. Hearts broke.

The mother asked me what to do. Sometimes there aren't enough hugs. I encouraged her to prayerfully appoint three or four women to be restorers to her daughter. These had to be women who weren't afraid to talk about sin and were willing to spend some time bearing the burden. The mother organized a special night of prayer devoted just to her daughter. Together the little band of women revisited the sexual sin and prayed over the young woman for complete healing and release from any unholy bonds. They prayed over her broken heart, too, and helped her to pray forgiveness over that young man who'd walked away. In the weeks and months to come, this core group of women began to re-dream with her. They were the secret of the Lord for her! Last I heard, the girl was engaged to a man who was more familiar with the fact that forgiveness actually means what it says . . . giving yourself for another! And he was planning to do that for the rest of his life!

On the contrary, last summer I counseled with a college-aged girl who is a mom by now. As I sat with her, I realized that she was in shock. She recounted how she and her fiancé, both students at a Christian college, had engaged in sexual intercourse once in the winter. Distraught, they confessed to her parents and to his. They wanted accountability. I've not heard of many so bravely moved to a righteous response to sin. Wow! But in the spring, passion got the best of them, and they chose sexual sin once again. This time, she became pregnant. The couple decided to keep the baby and give up their dreams of finishing school. Several members of her Christian family were suddenly and obviously avoiding her. Her pastor explained that she and her fiancé could not be married in their church. Her Christian school didn't welcome her back. She didn't know which way to turn or what to do.

Let me emphasize that this was a godly young woman who'd grown up serving God and who deeply desired to do the right thing. The familiar places she most thought she could find help to make it through were the places that created the deepest wounds. I'm ashamed of congregations and Christian organizations that operate under written rules of discipline without any allowance for measuring the sinner's brokenness and repentance. While I realize an unrepentant heart requires discipline, one broken by sin deserves restoration!

If I hear one more person defend kicking a girl out of her Christian school for pregnancy on the basis of protecting the rest of the flock, I think I'll scream! Remember reading in Chapter 1 how the Christian teen sexuality rate rivals the sexuality rate of unchurched teens? Well, the abortion rate among Christian women compared to the rate for our nonreligious peers shows little difference in the way we live our lives. Obviously something isn't working.

I'm deeply touched by the courage of Christine A. Scheller, who wrote about her choice to bring life out of her crisis pregnancy when she was in college. She moved on to graduate from college as a single mom, to be married, and to minister in many powerful ways. She writes,

... in our churches we so often talk about abortion as if it were an evil separate from us. But unless we are honest with ourselves about who we are, we cannot hope to turn our own culture on its head, let alone influence the larger one. One story suffices to describe it: My husband and I befriended a young woman years ago when he was a student at a Christian University. I was ripe with my second pregnancy when she abruptly disappeared from our lives. Several months later she reappeared with an explanation. She had had successive sexual relationships with two Bible college students. She had gotten pregnant by a youth leader of a church. He had driven her to the abortion clinic, paid to get rid of the problem—wouldn't even go inside with her—then dropped her off at her dorm when it was over. She said she thought I would understand, and she knew God would forgive her. She continued serving in various ministries, graduated with her class, and married into a respected Christian family.

I attended her bridal shower, but I didn't "understand" for some time. I was angry at the perceived injustice of others "getting away with" their sin while mine was costly and public. The anger subsided, and I began to feel sorry for her as I recalled my exquisite experience of the grace of God: A laughing child in exchange for sin. How incomparable![1]

A laughing child in exchange for sin. Let us be the church that creates a safe place for more women to know this grace.

RESTORE THE REPENTANT

The apostle Paul makes a startling statement in 1 and 2 Corinthians about our canned policies for discipline. In 1 Corinthians, Paul tells the church in Corinth to turn their backs on a man who is having sex with his father's wife. He tells them to excommunicate him. But guess what? In 2 Corinthians Paul admonishes the church to restore the same man to the full rights and privileges of membership. Yep, that's right! The incestuous adulterer is restored back into his place. Bible scholars believe this is because Paul is given news of the man's brokenness and repentance. Guess how much time passes between these two letters? A few months.

> *"We don't have to be rocket scientists to figure out that Satan's favorite prey is a person of godly influence . . . Not everyone in a stronghold of sin is having a good time."*[2]
> —BETH MOORE

Friend, as the secret of the Lord, we are uniquely equipped and required to walk with those whose maskless faces have revealed sin. Whether they choose to take those masks off or they're ripped away, you and I are called to be the secret of the Lord . . . to gently and truthfully restore . . . to re-dream with them! To isolate the loneliness, not them. Although I do realize that the process of restoration sometimes begins with discipline, I'm very concerned with the fact that it seems to be where we end, too. Let us not finish halfway. Let us restore those who display repentant hearts. Let us free others in the church to tell their rescue stories by telling our own.

God uses our stories. Your story is the only thing that is truly unique to you. It is intricately wrapped into your relationship with the body of Christ and your power to serve Him. To not share the highs and lows is to deny God's hand in it . . . and to steal from others the story's power to heal.

The secret of the Lord is all about telling our stories. But we are not easily encouraged to tell our stories. We fear man.

When we learn to fear God and speak of His rescue, we will find a treasure, the secret of the Lord. Our stories are the key of the door to this great adventure.

SHOULD I WALK WITH MEN WHO ARE LONELY?

As I encourage you to walk with others who are faced with the horrid pain of sin, I want to also caution you. Galatians 6:1 not only encourages us to walk with fallen believers, but it also admonishes, "Watch yourself, or you also may be tempted." Certainly, this addresses our need to be humble in confronting or disciplining a broken believer. It can also be applied to our need to be cautious about falling into sin ourselves. Although there are many realms of sin that you'll need to love fallen believers through, the intimacy required in any such relationship could lead to an emotional or physical intimacy that is inappropriate when a woman walks with a man. I believe that women should walk with women. Intimacy is a powerful emotional elixir. In my own life, I would not mix it in the presence of another man. No matter how unattractive or unlikely an emotional or a physical attraction might seem, I simply avoid all gray areas. I'm never alone with another man, nor do I talk with one about intimate issues. I have extremely high boundaries concerning this. I recommend that you do as well.

∞— It's Your Turn —∞

I hope that the Lord has brought to your mind someone who needs you. If He did, write in your journal a prayer for her and let God reveal to you how you should begin to walk beside her. If no one came to mind, begin with some silence before you write. Ask God to open your eyes to see the person who needs you to minister the secret of the Lord to her.

CHAPTER FOURTEEN

Revival

The thief comes only to steal and kill and destroy;
I have come that they may have life,
and have it to the full.

—JOHN 10:10

*R*rrrrring"

"Hello, this is Dannah," I answered the phone just a few weeks ago.

It was a director from a well-known international compassion ministry. He said they were starting a movement in one of their key countries. They had a vision to hold their first stadium event this year to fight HIV/AIDS and had hoped to hold multiple events in coming years, saturating that nation with truth about sexuality and purity. They wanted to know if Bob and I would come in November to be the keynote speakers .

"What country?" I asked, having never been extended a speaking opportunity in a foreign nation.

"Zambia," he replied.

Irony? I don't think so. In fact, their first choice had turned them down. We were second string. Though the agency knew little about our passion for this infrequently named African nation, God knew.

A call to purpose? Most definitely.

I'm silly with excitement that the very same month this book is released, I'll be catching my second flight to Zambia. Apparently, the dream is bigger than just one visit. In fact, this trip opens up the door to another next year in which we'll build a piggery and a fishery to financially support our friends John and Wisdom and the others as they teach in the government schools. God apparently thinks these two middle-aged writers and administrators have farming skills to learn.

I don't know what's beyond that. God's still writing my life story. Day by day. Page by page. Adventure by adventure.

My God loves to bless me. Because I know Him so intimately, I say this with full assurance. He is always surprising me with wonderful gifts. That's simply part of His covenant. We can't end our time together in these pages without one last peek into the heart of the secret of the Lord, the covenant.

Covenant is a complex, difficult to explain relationship. It is the great romance between Creator and creation. It's the special promises extended only to the body of Christ—the secret of the Lord. It's God versus Satan slugging it out over you.

It's the blood on the cross, the mediation of Christ on man's behalf, the absolute dying of ourselves into a life of slavery to that Savior . . . not because we *have to* serve Him but because love absolutely compels us.

It begins when you surrender your life to Christ.

And it ends . . . well, that's what is so exciting . . . the end of covenant. The result. If you recall, I mentioned that covenant always ends in blessings when we are committed to live under the obligations of it. For us as New Testament believers, it results in life . . . no, not just life . . . but abundant life!

John 10:10 says, "The thief comes only to steal and kill and destroy; I have come that they may have life, and have it to the full."

In some versions, that last phrase says that Jesus Christ came that we can have "abundant life."

Abundant life!

Not I'm-so-exhausted, depleted, empty, and depressed life. Not even I'm-just-makin'-it life. And certainly, this doesn't describe masses of believers merely existing in spiritual comas. Nope, these are believers who have known God's reviving power.

Abundant life!

That means a life that exceeds your dreams . . . that goes beyond what you've expected . . . that fills you up to the fullest. I cannot help but point out that I was once hoping God could fix my heart just enough to enable me to be used in maybe one or two lives in my church or neighborhood. I was spiritually weary and broken. (But I *looked* good . . . picture perfect!) Today, I let all my blood-covered—as in Christ has covered them—scars out in the open for others to see. I may not *look* as good, but I'm alive! I've been revived, and—God only knows how this is possible—this year tens of thousands of teenagers will be taught abstinence skills using books I have written and events I have developed. From my little town of State College, Pennsylvania, to the faraway home of my heart, Ndola, Zambia. I asked God for a few lives. He's giving me tens of thousands. I'm doing things I never dreamed of simply because I told my story and allowed God to spiritually revive me.

LIFE!

When we make salvation only about eternal life in heaven, we offer only half of the picture, and we rob ourselves of the understanding of covenant. I think salvation is about eternal life, but I think eternal life includes *now* life, too. It's about living a full and fulfilling life on this earth. It's a life that's filled to overflowing with mind-boggling blessings.

Malcolm Smith, author of *The Lost Secret of the New Covenant,* has forever changed my perception of death. He explains that God stated a factual truth to Adam and Eve about the tree of the knowledge of good and evil when He said, "The day you eat of it you shall surely die!" Did they in fact die *that* day? Smith writes:

> The problem with defining death is that those who are in the state of death are doing the defining and are convinced that they are alive! From their perspective, they are alive now and death is what happens at the end of physical life; but the Bible plainly says that outside of Christ, they are not alive now! This is the world of the walking dead who do not live but exist.[1]

I believe his opinion is well supported by Scripture. Remember, Jesus told Jairus that his daughter was not dead, but she was asleep. He apparently looked with spiritual eyes. Take a peek with me at a couple of verses that refer to the death and life of New Testament believers.

"As for you, you were dead in your transgressions and sins . . .
But because of his great love for us, God, who is rich in
mercy, made us alive with Christ even when we were dead . . ."
—EPHESIANS 2:1, 4–5

This is why [the Scripture] said,
"Wake up, O sleeper, rise from the dead,
and Christ will shine on you."
—EPHESIANS 5:14

Yes, indeed, we misunderstand death. Our definition is wrong.

Those who exist without Christ are dead. But I'm afraid that all too often, those of us who are offered the blessing of abundant life aren't fully alive. We stay mired down in the trappings of this world. We hide behind our masks, stuffing the story that releases us to victory into a deep, dark corner. We are the existing dead. We live in spiritual comas.

I have gone from being a ghost of a believer to being very much alive. I've found passion, and I'm living in a dream so much bigger than myself. Oh, how I want this for you. Oh, how God in His great love wants it for you. Reach for it.

You were meant to live abundantly. Reach for it.

Tell your story.

Wait on God to see how He will use it. Let Him revive you and fill you with His power.

YADA! YADA! YADA!

Oh, that brings me to a point of squealing with delight. Forgive me for getting giddy, but my precious God just thrills me beyond my wildest dreams. I was sitting here tonight laboring over one of my favorite chapters, the chapter on "yada." Remember a few chapters back when we got on that bunny trail about sex? We discussed *yada,* the word that talks of an intimate knowing, that special, shameless oneness between husband and wife, as well as the mighty, spine-tingling knowing of our precious God.

Well, tonight God called me back to that chapter. I was confused. I felt we had "yada" covered, but the Lord would not release me. He was clearly calling me to go back to study the Hebrew word more thoroughly. (This *was* "yada," incidentally. I knew His voice. I didn't hear it, but I sensed it.) As I pored over the nearly nine hundred occurrences of "yada" in the Old Testament, my eyes fell upon a verse I'd somehow missed during this entire writing process . . . until this very night.

Guess what I found? "The secret of the LORD is with those who fear him and he makes his covenant known [*yada*] to them."

Can I scream with delight?

Oh, how God has truly written this book page by page, paragraph by paragraph. I cannot take credit for this wonderful surprise revelation. I had no idea! But I do believe God has saved the best for last so that I can just revel in His handiwork. Will you join me? (Yes, go ahead and stand up and holler! I am!)

Oh, my sweet friend, until we know Him, we cannot truly live. It all comes back to sitting at His feet, whispering His name, worshipping Him in awe and wonder every single day of our lives. When we are so close to God that we can feel His breath, we can truly live. Oh, join me in knowing Him. He'll do the rest. We just need to know Him!

Oh, I'm living. I want more life, but I'm living!

I'm living every moment I share an "aha" moment of learning with my sweet daughter, Lexi. I'm living every moment I cuddle into my husband's warmth at night. I'm living every moment as I watch my Robby become a godly man.

I'm living when I watch the sun rise on an African safari. I'm living when I watch it rise on my sweet Pennsylvania mountain.

I'm living when I counsel a girl whose heart is tempted by sexual sin. (I'm really living when I get an invitation to her wedding years later and she's waited!)

I'm living; oh, I'm living . . . when I hear from my precious friends in Zambia. I cannot describe how this feels. It is like no pleasure I have ever known in my life. Nothing delights my heart more than when our Zambian director, John Banda, sends me photos of volunteers speaking truth, sharing dreams, hopes, fears . . . being the secret of the Lord in every way.

Wisdom has continued to speak when his body is strong enough to get around. He travels with the Pure Freedom team to spread truth about HIV/AIDS and to offer the truth of abstinence and God's great forgiveness. His courage has created courage in others who have found healing from him and in sharing their own stories about struggling with HIV/AIDS. Telling his story strikes holy fear into the Zambian teens who otherwise feel immune to this once faceless horror. Telling his story breathes strength into those already plagued by the disease.

Wisdom has found the secret of the Lord and can now be part of the secret.

Oh, that we could follow his brave example and send our masks crashing to the ground. Instead of these ugly masks, let us wear the cloak of the covenant.

Some say Wisdom is dying. I say he is finally living. He would say that as well.

Oh, I'm living! Join me! Join Wisdom!

Live!

PURE FREEDOM

Visit my ministry Web site at www.purefreedom.org. Bob and I are shameless about sharing our love for Africa. You'll be able to see what new project God has laid on our hearts for the people of Zambia. Maybe it'll inspire you as you "re-dream."

Endnotes

An Invitation to Revival

1. C. S. Lewis, *The Pilgrim's Regress* (Grand Rapids: Eerdmans, 1981 ed.), 5.
2. Foreword by Larry Crabb in Randy Frazee, *The Connecting Church* (Grand Rapids, MI: Zondervan, 2001), 13.
3. Reggie McNeal, *The Present Future* (San Francisco: Jossey-Bass, 2003), 3–4.
4. Barna Research Online, "Most People Seek Control, Adventure and Peace for Their Lives" (Ventura, CA: Barna Research, 1 August 2000) www.barna.org/cgi-bin/PagePressRelease.asp?PressReleaseID=68& Reference=E&Key=loneliness.
5. Cheryl K. Ewings, "When Depression Hits Home," *Today's Christian Woman*, December 1999, http://www.christianitytoday.com/tcw/9w6/9w6090.html.

Chapter 1: Prepare to Re-Dream

1. Beth Moore, *Beloved Disciple Bible Study Workbook* (Nashville: Lifeway, 2002), 143.
2. www.barna.org, "The Year's Most Intriguing Findings from Barna Research Studies," posted 12 December 2000, Barna Research Online.
3. Joshua Mann, M.D., M.P.H., Joe S. McIlhaney, Jr., M.D., and Curtis C. Stine, M.D., *Building Healthy Futures* (Austin, TX: The Medical Institute, 2000), 5.
4. www.barna.org, "Morality Continues to Decay," posted 3 November 2003, Barna Research Online.
5. www.barna.org, "Practical Outcomes Replace Biblical Principles as the Moral Standard," posted 10 September 2001, Barna Research Online.

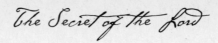

6. The Leadership Survey on Pastors and Pornography, http://www.ctlibrary.com/le/2001/winter/12.89.html.

7. Bruce Wilkinson, *Beyond Jabez* (Sisters, OR: Multnomah, 2005), 194.

8. Ibid., 195.

Chapter 2: Prepare to Awaken the Enemy

1. Robert Fitts, *The Church in the House: A Return to Simplicity* (Salem, OR: Preparing the Way Publishers, 2001), 16.

2. Brother Yun with Paul Hattaway, *The Heavenly Man* (Mill Hill, London: Monarch Books, 2002), 223.

3. Ibid., 163–64.

4. Neil T. Anderson and Dave Park, *The Bondage Breaker: Youth Edition* (Eugene, OR: Harvest House, 2001), 13.

5. Neil T. Anderson, *The Bondage Breaker* (Eugene, OR: Harvest House, 1990), 20.

Chapter 3: A Prescription for Loneliness

1. Randy Frazee, *The Connecting Church* (Grand Rapids, MI: Zondervan, 2001), 22.

2. Tim Stafford, "A Heaven-Made Activist," *Christianity Today,* January 2004, 50.

Chapter 4: Lie #1: "I'm All Alone Here!"

1. James Bryan Smith, *An Arrow Pointing to Heaven* (Nashville: Broadman & Holman, 2000), 174.

2. Nancy Leigh DeMoss, *Brokenness: The Heart God Revives* (Chicago: Moody Publishers, 2002), 143.

3. Brennan Manning, *The Ragamuffin Gospel* (Sisters, OR: Multnomah, 2000), 85.

4. Philip Yancey, "Lessons from Rock Bottom," *Christianity Today,* 10 July 2000, back page.

5. Manning, *The Ragamuffin Gospel*, 84.

Chapter 5: Lie #2: "There's No One I Can Talk To"
1. Beth Moore, *To Live Is Christ* (Nashville: Lifeway, 1997), 124.
2. Tammy Maltby, *Lifegiving* (Chicago: Moody Publishers, 2002), 40.
3. Beth Moore, *When Godly People Do Ungodly Things Bible Study* (Nashville: Lifeway, 2003), 20.

Chapter 6: Lie #3: "God Has No Use for Me Now"
1. Moore, *Beloved Disciple Bible Study Workbook*, 68.
2. Jack Hayford, *Living the Spirit-Formed Life* (Ventura, CA: Regal Books, 2001), 136.

Chapter 7: The Fear of Man
1. Malcolm Smith, *The Lost Secret of the New Covenant* (Tulsa, OK: Harrison House, 2002), 272.
2. Brother Yun and Hattaway, *The Heavenly Man*, 313.

Chapter 8: The Fear of God
1. Nancy Leigh DeMoss, *Surrender* (Chicago: Moody Publishers, 2003), 166.
2. John Eldredge, *Waking the Dead* (Nashville: Thomas Nelson Publishers, 2003), 166.

Chapter 9: The Reward of Fearing God
1. Matt Redman, *The Unquenchable Worshipper* (Ventura, CA: Regal Books, 2001), 50–51.

Chapter 10: Yada! Yada! Yada!
1. Watchman Nee, *Sit, Walk, Stand* (Wheaton, IL: Tyndale, 1977), 14.
2. Lewis A. Drummond, *The Evangelist* (Nashville: Word, 2001), 17–20.

3. Mark R. McMinn, *Why Sin Matters* (Wheaton, IL: Tyndale, 2004), 53.

Chapter 11: Covenant Power

1. Kay Arthur, *Our Covenant God* (Colorado Springs: Waterbrook Press, 1999), 171.
2. Brother Yun and Hattaway, *Heavenly Man*, 298–99.
3. Erlo Stegan, *Revival Among the Zulus* (Kranskop, South Africa: Khanya Press, 1998), 4–5.
4. www.christianitytoday.com/ct/2000/009/1.40.html, Missions & Ministry column.

Chapter 12: The Hem of His Garment

1. A. W. Tozer, *Rut, Rot, or Revival* (Camp Hill, PA: Christian Publications, 1993), 2–3.

Chapter 13: Walking with the Maskless

1. Christine A. Scheller, "A Laughing Child in Exchange for Sin," *Christianity Today,* February 2004, http://www.christianitytoday.com/ct/2004/002/6.54.html.
2. Beth Moore, *When Godly People Do Ungodly Things* (Nashville: Broadman & Holman, 2002), 12–13.

Chapter 14: Revival

1. Smith, *The Lost Secret of the New Covenant*, 28.

$\mathcal{D}$annah Gresh remembers well the moment that God wrote a mission statement on her heart. She was walking through the windy city of Chicago when it was revealed from above. "Your mission is to equip men and women of all ages to live a vibrant life of purity, to experience healing from past impurity if it exists in their lives, and to experience a vibrant, passionate marriage that portrays the love Christ has for his Bride, the church." It was breathed into her, word for word, exactly like that, and she has never forgotten it. Dannah remembers hearing God's voice so vibrantly and yet ... she had no platform, no connections, no "ministry." Just a specific life call to be something very different from the over-worked marketing consultant she was at the time.

That was eight years ago. Today, Dannah is the author of the best-selling *And the Bride Wore White*, which has touched the lives of over 200,000 teens and college-aged women. She is also the author of the best-selling Secret Keeper series and the creator of Pure Freedom retreats and the Secret Keeper Girl Tour.

Most exciting to Dannah is when God called her to Africa in

2002. Again, she said, "I don't know a single soul on that continent, Lord." For two years, Dannah and her husband, Bob, prayed for God to open a door in Africa if it were His will. In 2004, God did just that. With no one else but Dannah's mom knowing of their prayer, they were invited to develop a curriculum to be used in the seventy-two government schools of Zambia, Africa—a nation that has a 16–22 percent rate of HIV/AIDS infection and in which 10 percent of the population is orphaned due to AIDS. Nearly 100,000 Zambian teens will receive the message of purity and God's love through Pure Freedom Zambia, a ministry which is entirely operated by natives in Zambia whom Bob and Dannah train.

In 2006, the Greshes will help build a piggery/fishery to fund the work in Zambia and within five years, with God's help, will build a Christian school to house and educate 100 orphans.

Bob Gresh is the founder of Grace Prep Christian high school, a new model in Christian education, where Dannah teaches Real World Living (health from a Christian worldview) and which will be the sister school of the Zambian Grace Prep.

Bob and Dannah live in State College, Pennsylvania with their children, Robby and Lexi, and their very adorable labradoodle, Stormie.